Charles E Nicholson

AND HIS YACHTS

Charles E Nicholson

AND HIS YACHTS

Franco Pace
text by *William Collier*

ADLARD COLES NAUTICAL
London

Acknowledgements
Franco Pace would like to thank the owners,
skippers and crews of all the yachts featured
and L'Associazione Italiana Vele D'Epoca.

Published 2000 by Adlard Coles Nautical
an imprint of A & C Black (Publishers) Ltd
35 Bedford Row, London WC1R 4JH
www.adlardcoles.co.uk

First published in Italy by Edizione Reporter in 2000

ISBN 0–7136–5736–7

A CIP catalogue record for this book is available from the British Library.

Photographs (except pages 6–21) by Franco Pace
Photographs, pages 6–2: William Collier
Text by William Collier: pages 6–21, 22–3, 54–5,
90–1, 132–3, 142–3, 154–5
All other text by Franco Pace and William Collier

Typeset in 11 on 14pt Galliard
Printed and bound in Italy.

Note: All specifications given at the beginning of the yacht portraits
refer to the original design of the yacht when it was launched.

Contents

Charles E Nicholson
and his yachts

Charles E Nicholson became recognised as a force within yacht design at a time when his father's firm was in decline. Although only formed as Camper & Nicholson in 1863, the Gosport-based yacht builders were the direct continuation of the yard established in the latter part of the 18th century by Frances Calense Amos. In 1809 Amos was joined by his great-nephew William Camper, who became an apprentice in his yard and eventually took it over in 1824. It was Camper who forged strong links with the wealthy members of the Royal Yacht Squadron and positioned the business at the forefront of the emergent yacht building industry. From the launching of the cutter *Breeze* in 1836 onwards, Camper built up a reputation as a builder of fast yachts. For a twenty-year period he built a large number of yachts, particularly schooners which were favoured by a prestigious clientele, and so his name was well established by the mid-nineteenth century. The trauma of *America*'s 1851 defeat of the cream of British yachts in the founding race for the America's Cup, followed in 1854 by the outbreak of the Crimean War and the consequent cessation of yachting heralded a premature decline to Camper's career.

The interruption by war left the many questions raised about *America*'s apparent superiority in abeyance and it was not until 1860 that a new British schooner, the *Aline*, appeared to offer an innovative design solution. *Aline*'s designer and builder was Ben Nicholson, who had joined Camper's yard as a shipwright apprentice in 1842. Thanks to a combination of skill and the lack of a clear male heir

within the Camper family, Nicholson had risen to become the senior employee. *Aline*'s incredible racing success prompted Nicholson's further promotion and facilitated his choice as Camper's replacement when the latter sought to retire in 1863. Financed by both Camper and the Lapthorn family, who operated the sail loft adjacent to the yard, Nicholson not only took over Camper's business but also undertook a 30-year programme of expansion. In tonnage terms, the design and construction of large schooners dominated the firm's output, and to this staple Nicholson added an extensive refit and maintenance business which was made possible by the near constant expansion of the yard's facilities.

Nicholson's business agenda was deeply influenced by his appreciation of the factors that had curtailed William Camper's career. Design ability fuelled demand for new yachts, but this expertise was always liable to be subjected to unpredictable assault, and the demand for yachts would always be at the mercy of wider-scale political and economic factors. By broadening the base of his business Nicholson isolated himself from such vagaries and by the mid-1880s, when his own design ability was successfully challenged by emergent designers like G L Watson and the third William Fife, he had created a firm whose future was no longer dependent on design ability. Henceforth he anticipated that external designers would be able to provide the designs for his yard to build, and it needed simply to rely on its well established reputation for quality construction and maintenance. As to his sons, whilst Ben Nicholson

welcomed them into the firm, and added the 's' to Camper & Nicholson in 1895 to signal their arrival, he never encouraged them to develop the design skills that he had succeeded in marginalising within his business. Of the three sons who entered the business, Nicholson planned that the eldest, Benjamin junior (born 1852), should take over the management, that Charles E Nicholson (born 1868) should become a salesman, and to this end had him partly educated in France so as to increase his language base, and that the youngest, Arthur W Nicholson (born 1871), should become a real estate agent and thus take care of the family's property holdings. The subsequent emergence of Charles as an immensely talented yacht designer forced a revision of Nicholson's plans.

Dating the exact start of Charles E Nicholson's design career is made difficult by the conflicting evidence he left. In 1895 he wrote: '*After school days I started in this business where I learned what I know of yacht building and designing, the responsibility of which I took over ten years ago at the time my father gave up the board.*' By 1901, however, he stated rather more plausibly that he had '*done the designing for the firm during the last ten years*'. Despite these apparent contradictions, there is consensus that his first design to be commercially built was the small cutter *Lucifer* in 1887. It is also clear from available evidence that C E Nicholson's early career was not entirely devoted to designing. In the same decade that he assumed the role of company designer he also '*superintended the building and repair work*'. Thus his education might be characterised as that of a good all-rounder.

In 1889 the most important yacht built by the yard was certainly the smallest. That year leading yachtsman Sir Hercules Langrishe had been instrumental in founding the informal and short-lived Yachts' Boat Sailing Association, which organised races for the small boats carried on board yachts. To compete in these activities Langrishe commissioned C E Nicholson to design and build a sailing replacement for the four-oared gig formerly carried on his cutter *Samoena*. Travelling to ports throughout England, Scotland and Ireland on board the mother ship, this 20-foot cutter proved to be able to beat anything of her length and

became a mobile advertisement for the young designer. By 1891 the success of this small boat translated into more important work, with Nicholson securing two design and build commissions. Nicholson also capitalised on his French education and obtained the commission to design and build the cruiser *Guimili* for a French aristocrat. The second commission was for the small racing yacht *Coquette*, very similar in type to *Samoena*'s cutter but built as a two and a half Rater under the Yacht Racing Association's (YRA) 1886 Length and Sail Area Rule. That year Langrishe had ordered the Fife-designed 5 Rater *Iernia*, built by Camper & Nicholsons, but in the light of *Coquette*'s success he replaced her with the Nicholson-designed *Dacia* the following year. This was just one of seven racing designs commissioned from Nicholson for the 1892 season, orders all apparently inspired by *Coquette*'s successes. As early as May 1892 Charles E Nicholson was described as '*exceptionally lucky with this year's new raters*', and this was followed by the '*astounding rumour*' that *Dacia* had been well sold by Langrishe to his yachting friend the Earl of Dudley for

£1,000 (twice her original cost). His reputation was further enhanced when *Dacia*, under the flag of her new owner and helmed by her designer, beat *Natica*, the G L Watson-designed favourite in a specially arranged match series for high stakes. On *Dacia*'s first race Nicholson had sailed with Langrishe who later recalled that: '*He* [Nicholson] *had build a splendid reaching boat to please me, but he was very doubtful about her windward work. Well, he had turned out a champion on a wind too, and he couldn't believe it! Dacia that year won fourteen firsts in fourteen starts.*' Nicholson's successes in the 1892 season were enough to catapult him unexpectedly to the forefront of British yacht design.

The pace with which Nicholson achieved early and widespread recognition and patronage was directly linked to his father's status and the access that this gave him to leading yachting patrons. With just a small number of significant clients the results he achieved were outstanding, as the following example illustrates. After acquiring the 5 Rater *Dacia* in 1892, the Earl of Dudley commissioned the larger 20 Rater *Vigorna* in 1893 because '*there are no prospects of a good 5 rating class on the Solent next season*'. When she proved to be a failure he replaced her the following year with another 20 Rater, *Inyoni*. Langrishe, having sold *Dacia* to Dudley, went on to build three further Nicholson designs in 1893–94. Thus, from one successfully completed commission, there were five directly attributable orders. Although not universally successful, C E Nicholson's designs enabled

PREVIOUS DOUBLE PAGE: *Camper & Nicholsons' laying-up yard in Gosport in 1912.*

LEFT: *C E Nicholson inspecting progress on the construction of the racing schooner* Margherita.

ABOVE: *Charles E Nicholson 1868–1954.*

FOLLOWING DOUBLE PAGE: *Charles E Nicholson at the helm of the Big Class cutter* Candida.

him to promote himself directly to other potential clients. Whilst he would later describe touting as '*a system I do not like and which I believe rarely helps a yacht builder*', he in fact used such an approach extensively to his direct advantage. Indeed the themes of his letters are generally similar. C E Nicholson systematically contacted yachtsmen, highlighting the possibilities or needs within a particular racing class and cited his design credentials. The needs that Nicholson identified were most frequently couched in terms of the desirability of representing '*South country designing and building in competition with the North*' at a time when the two most prestigious UK designers were the Scots William Fife Jnr and G L Watson. International competition gave even greater impetus to Nicholson's search for clients; the announcement that *Niagara*, designed by the American Nathaniel G Herreshoff, would compete in the UK in 1895

brought forth the following request to the Earl of Dudley to build a third 20 Rater in as many years:

'I fear none of the existing 20 Raters are good enough all round to meet the Herreshoff boat, and I am also aware that it is no easy matter to turn out a boat good enough to compete successfully with that Gentleman's clever productions, though thus this fact makes it all the more all English designers ambitions to have the opportunity to endeavour to do so, and I trust this will be sufficient reason for approaching your Lordship on the question of building another boat which I hope will not be considered as abusing the favours I have already received from you in this way.'

In the event Dudley did not order a new yacht and *Inyoni* beat the visitor, a fact that Nicholson was not slow to use in the search for further work. This was particularly the case when the opportunity occurred of challenging Herreshoff, the rival designer whose work he most admired. Whilst Herreshoff remained the designer of choice for America's Cup defenders, C E Nicholson sent what was probably his ultimate tout by telegraph directly to Lipton on board his steam yacht in New York immediately after the failure of the Watson-designed challenger *Shamrock II*:

'If intending further challenge and reports Watson not designing correct will you give me interview before placing order. Have reason to believe could beat existing 90 footers having beaten Herreshoff more than other British yacht designers with small yachts.'

Although C E Nicholson was not successful in securing an order for an America's Cup challenger until *Shamrock IV* in 1913, his touting methods served him well in obtaining considerable work in the smaller racing classes until the turn of the century.

For reasons inextricably bound up with commercial success and design prestige, it was important for Charles Nicholson to join his designing peers, Fife, Watson and Herreshoff, in the production of larger sailing yachts. Despite potentially attractive financial conditions offered by the yard, good connections and extensive touting, this ambition was initially marred by his rather maverick performance. After the success of his 1892 designs, when three commissions in the two and a half Rater class had enabled him to conduct experiments with three different keel types, Nicholson adopted the fin and bulb keel configuration and turned his attention to hull forms. In 1893 he adopted very radical shallow-draft, flat 'skimming dish' hulls with the proven keel type for all his designs. The resultant *Vigorna*, then the largest 'fin and bulb' type yacht built in the country, was the most notable of that year's many Nicholson-designed failures. For the emergent designer the commercial implications were clear: '*This is a*

very serious matter to me, as my reputation as a designer is only of a very few seasons standing and I am most anxious to follow up this part of our business especially.'

After 1894 Nicholson's racing yachts performed more consistently, but the particular and complex circumstances of the UK yacht racing environment in the latter 1890s did not favour his chances of obtaining a commission for a large yacht. In 1896 the introduction of a new rating rule, the First Linear Rating Rule, was designed to curb the excesses possible under the old rule, which Nicholson had so successfully exploited, but it also put virtually all the racing tonnage built prior to 1896 at great disadvantage. The most famous instance of the consequent disenchantment with yacht racing was that of the Prince of Wales, who withdrew his first class cutter, the 1893 Watson-designed *Britannia*, from racing in 1897 since she could not compete with the German Kaiser's newly built *Meteor II*. Rather than alleviating the problems encountered under the old rule, its replacement heralded another period of rapid and extreme design evolution where from year to year new yachts were outclassed and rendered useless for racing. One side effect was to herald the inception of a large number of one design and restricted classes, of which C E Nicholson's first Bembridge Redwing class of 1897 was typical. Another was a prudent tendency by owners to build to the smaller yacht classes, where Nicholson fared well.

In response to the problems the new rule caused, the YRA abandoned class racing to allow yachts of greatly varying sizes to race together on a handicap basis. The result was an unsatisfactory hybrid handicap class in which greatest advantage was achieved by building extremely light yachts, as exemplified by the Watson-designed *Kariad*. These lightly built yachts had no future as cruising yachts beyond their racing lives. With virtually no resale value and little possibility of recouping a significant proportion of the building costs, they further contributed to the demise of first class yacht racing. At the height of the handicap era Charles Nicholson secured the order for his first large yacht, the yawl *Brynhild* of 1899. Her owner died at the end of her first season, but after being acquired by Sir James Pender *Brynhild* began a successful racing career in the handicap class. Her success boded well for C E Nicholson, but in the continuing vacuum he was only able to secure his next commission for a similar type cruiser/racer in 1904. Again because of extraneous circumstances, the resultant *Merrymaid* changed hands at the end of her first season. After a successful second season her new owner Robert W N Young decided to go in for a larger yacht and considered acquiring *Kariad*. The suggestion was anathema to Nicholson, who had published an article on the decline of first class racing in that year.

As Young was willing to buy a larger yacht, Nicholson seized the opportunity to lead by example. He highlighted the many disadvantages that would result from acquiring *Kariad* and expressed the hope that, instead, his firm might be chosen to build a new yacht. The premature claim that the introduction of scantling regulations by the

YRA was imminent convinced his customer. With the prin-ciple of a new yacht approved on these grounds, Nicholson easily convinced Young that this vessel should be built 'to obtain a high class at Lloyd's'. When the strong, seaworthy and fast *Nyria* appeared in 1906 she was acclaimed as a great success. For the international committee sitting to agree the First International Rating Rule during 1906 *Nyria* provided an example to follow and in January 1907 the new rule, inclusive of Lloyd's Register (R class) scant-ling regulations, came into force for ten years. This provid-ed a resolution of the crisis in large yacht racing that had last-ed a decade, in a manner that wholly vindicated Nicholson.

With the subsequent breaking up of *Kariad* the last vestiges of the supremacy that G L Watson held over UK yacht design in the last two decades of the nineteenth century were gone. Although in the final years of his career Watson had concentrated on steam yacht design, which his firm continued to prioritise after his death, his passing in 1904 broke the stranglehold that he and fellow Scotsman William Fife Jnr had held over UK yacht design. Now Nicholson could claim to be Fife's rival.

Nicholson had progressively built up the tonnage of cruising yacht commissions obtained by the yard, but these were only increased significantly after the successes of his first large racing yachts. *Almara* and *Lista* followed *Nyria* in 1907, the yet larger *Pampa* followed the 1907 *Brynhild II*, and the process culminated in the construction of the two large schooners *Sylvana* (now *Orion*) and *La Cigale* between late 1909 and the spring of 1910. Some earlier cruising yacht customers, such as Fred Milburn, for whom *Norlanda* was built in 1905, graduated with C E Nicholson into the sphere of large racing yachts in late 1910, having been offered one of two 19 Metre class yachts being built by Fife. Milburn forwarded Nicholson details of these vessels and commis-sioned *Norada*, a Camper & Nicholsons-built rival. Beyond the commercial importance of building a 100 ton TM (Thames Measurement) yacht, by 1911 the 19 Metre class had become the focus of large yacht racing. It superseded the 23 Metre class, which had been reduced to only two con-tenders after the accidental sinking of *Brynhild II* in 1910. In a class of four yachts, two of which were designed by Fife and one by Mylne, Nicholson's status was also considerably enhanced by *Norada*'s good performance. In 1912 emphasis shifted to the 15 Metre class with the Nicholson-designed and built *Istria*. The first use of the so-called 'Marconi' rig, laminated wood construction and a radical design enabled her to dominate a class in which Nicholson had no prior experience. The seven yachts that Fife had contributed to the class up to 1912, as well as the four from Mylne's draughting board, were outclassed. The success of *Istria* led directly to the ordering of sister 15 Metres, *Pamela* and *Paula III*, which joined *Istria* in a class that became totally dominated by Nicholson-designed and built yachts.

ABOVE: *The afterguard, or team of advisors, including Charles Nicholson, on board* Margherita *at Kiel Week in 1913.*

In numerical terms the 15 Metre class was by far the most important during this period. However, ultimate yachting prestige within Europe was derived from the even more rarefied sport of large schooner racing that had been reborn with the International Rule's A Class. Initially the class was dominated by the visiting American yacht *Westward,* specifically designed for European racing by Herreshoff. But, under the patronage of the German Kaiser, with his third and fourth *Meteor*s, and supported by a number of his courtiers, Germany assumed the lead in European schooner racing. With acquisition in 1908 of the 1902 Fife-designed schooner *Cicely*, the British yachtsman G Cecil Whitaker joined the schooner racing élite. However, *Cicely*, designed for handicap classes, was uncompetitive; as a patriot and motivated by an intense dislike of the Kaiser, Whitaker replaced her in 1911 with a new Fife design, *Waterwitch*. After an unsuccessful first season Whitaker turned to Nicholson who, respectful of professional etiquette, initially declined to undertake any alterations to the yacht. When eventually Nicholson agreed to intervene he was doubtful if any improvement could be great enough to beat the existing German schooners, and he was proved correct during the 1912 season when *Waterwitch* again fared badly. As a result, Nicholson made a '*much more drastic proposal*' which was, he claimed, '*chiefly prompted by the great disappointment shared by all interested in British yachting at seeing the Germans and Americans beat us in the A class. Your effort to uphold national prestige in this great sport deserved better success.*'

In the autumn of 1912 the drastic proposal of scrapping *Waterwitch* in favour of a new schooner to be designed and built by Nicholson, using as much as possible of the discarded vessel's gear, was given the go-ahead. For Nicholson, who had stated that his '*ambition should be attained*' in the event of securing such an order, the resultant *Margherita* not only vindicated his hopes by winning all except one race in 1913, but also established him as the leading British yacht designer. Even before the crowning achievements of *Margherita*, Charles Nicholson had already finally secured the ultimate yacht racing commission – the design of an America's Cup challenger. But when *Shamrock IV* was in mid-Atlantic, on passage to New York and the race series, World War I erupted, leaving Nicholson to comment that this '*terrible reality ... at once obliterated* Shamrock, *the unimportance of such matters having wiped out any regrets one would have keenly felt at a postponement under any other circumstances.*'

The First World War could not have come at a worse time for Nicholson: he appeared to be at the height of his career, had recently doubled the capacity of his yard by acquiring the old J G Fay & Co yard in Southampton and, more important, the social and business fabric that had led to a buoyant yachting scene was decimated by war. Yacht racing as such began again in 1920 but it was a pale immitation of the pre-1914 scene. The delayed *Shamrock IV* challenge for the America's Cup was fought and lost, whilst at home Nicholson gradually exerted his influence over the governing of yacht racing. In this he was greatly assisted by *Nyria*'s excellent performance, and at the end of that season her owner suggested yet further improving *Nyria*'s performance by converting her to the Marconi rig. In view of the heavy cost involved, Nicholson originally doubted the benefits of such an approach, but faced with an enthusiastic owner he suggested a more dramatic alteration. Thus in 1921 *Nyria* emerged with the first Bermudan rig ever fitted to a large racing yacht. It superseded the Marconi rig and introduced the most significant change in yacht rigging of the twentieth century. This, combined with successfully harmonising the handicaps applied to the Big Class yachts, allowed Nicholson to fully re-establish himself as the leading British yacht designer. But the crowning recognition of Nicholson's endeavours for the Big Class did not come until ten years after *Nyria*'s conversion, when George V commissioned Nicholson to convert *Britannia* to rate within the New York Yacht Club's (NYYC) Universal Rule. This required the royal cutter to be fitted with the largest Bermudan rig yet built. Its success was described as '*a monument to Nicholson's skill*'.

Attempts to reinvigorate the Big Class apart, Camper & Nicholsons' early post-war emphasis was on smaller racing yachts. Charles Nicholson's first post-First World War design was the Island Sailing Club's one design dinghy and, whilst

ABOVE: *Charles Nicholson at the helm of his yacht* Flame.
OPPOSITE: *The launch of the 1935 ocean racer* Foxhound.

this was of little economic consequence to his firm, it accorded with Nicholson's commitment to the overall interests of yachting. In fact yacht racing was to be reborn in the smaller classes such as the 6 Metres, and the firm's economic survival was far more linked to Nicholson's introduction of the diesel motor in power yachts and the manner in which he developed this new type than to the economically marginal vagaries of yacht racing. Camper & Nicholsons' new yard in Southampton soon became the world leader in motor yacht construction and after the last three large steam yachts were launched in 1930, Nicholson firmly established his dominance over the new type.

Motor yachts aside, it was the construction of auxiliary cruising yachts which first signalled Charles Nicholson's return to large sailing yacht design. Again design innovation in the 1920s consolidated the firm's expansion in this area. Despite Nicholson's pioneering first use of the Bermudan rig on the racing yacht *Nyria* in 1921, it did not lead to a unilateral adoption of the rig for cruising yachts. In 1923 he was still reserving his position on the matter and when he received the opportunity to design two cruising ketches in 1925 the developmental stage of his thinking was made clear. For the 78 ton Thames Measurement (TM) *Kathleen* he adopted the modern Bermudan rig, whilst for the larger 248 ton TM *Sylvia* he compromised, opting for Bermudan on the smaller mizzen mast and gaff rig on the main mast. *Sylvia* was converted a year later to full Bermudan rig, signalling the fact that Nicholson was finally close to settling his position by opting for an innovative approach to what was still a contentious question. However, the market for large auxiliary cruising yachts was a small one, and examples of the type being built in the period are relatively few. Indeed Nicholson's 132 ton TM *Blanche Neige* (now *Aile Blanche*), launched in 1939, was the last of the small number. The erosion of the auxiliary yacht market was largely caused by the fact that cruising yacht owners were unwilling to employ the crew numbers which even the more easily handled Bermudan rig required. In response to this Nicholson introduced the three-masted staysail schooner rig which in his words '*became a useful topic for conservative armchair yachting critics to deplore*'.

At 689 tons TM, the resultant *Vira* (now *Creole*) was the largest of all Nicholson's sailing yacht designs. The impact of *Vira* and her revolutionary rig in offering a new alternative in large sailing yacht design was virtually instant. Leading French yacht owner Virginie Heriot was directly inspired by *Vira* and immediately commissioned the construction of *Ailée*, in turn she was emulated by Marion B Carstairs who commissioned the near sister ship *Sonia II*.

Post-war class racing was initially dominated by the 6 Metre class, but in 1923 Fife was commissioned to design a 12 Metre and the emphasis began to ebb from the 6 Metres. Nicholson contributed *Clymene* and *Doris* to this class in 1924 and 1925 respectively, and it was once again in the ascendancy when it finally gained acceptance in America in 1927. At last there seemed to be a willingness

amongst owners to build to the larger classes. Confirmation came in 1928 when both Fife and Nicholson received orders for the 23 Metre Big Class cutters *Cambria* and *Astra*. Although these two orders appeared to confirm the seeming equality between the two designers, the intense competition between them was gradually being resolved. Fife's 6 Metre yachts had gained a narrow margin over Nicholson's. Conversely, Nicholson gained a moderate advantage in the 12 Metre class, which was greatly enhanced after the success of Sopwith's second 12 Metre, the 1928 *Mouette*. As a direct result, Sopwith's business rival Fairey exchanged the Fife 12 Metre *Modesty* for the new Nicholson-designed *Flica* in 1929, and Fife's position in the 12 Metre class was gradually eroded in Nicholson's favour.

With neither the 15 nor 19 Metre classes being recreated after World War I, the 12 Metre class was second only to the Big Class. Subject to the varying focus of racing activities, many owners such as Signer, Sopwith, Fairey and others shifted their allegiances between the two classes, and Nicholson's success in the 12 Metre class of the late 1920s led directly to Big Class commissions. In 1930 Nicholson gained Lipton's order for the J class America's Cup challenger *Shamrock V*, confirming his stranglehold over the British Big Class, of which Fife's 1928 *Cambria* was the only non-Nicholson designed constituent built in the inter-war period. Conversely, when Big Class racing collapsed after King George V's death in 1936, it was Nicholson not Fife who benefited from the consequent glut of 12 Metre orders.

Between 1930 and 1937 C E Nicholson designed, and Camper & Nicholsons built, four Big Class yachts to the American Universal Rule's J class rating; these were the only Big Class yachts built in Britain in the 1930s and they dominated first class racing in home waters. Nicholson's renewed involvement in the America's Cup went hand in hand with a resurgence of the ambiguous feelings that his first experience of this prestigious event had generated. The experience was a salutary one for Nicholson, and Lipton's death in 1931 brought an end to a further challenge that he had been planning. These factors apart, the 1930

ABOVE: *The interior of Camper & Nicholsons' building sheds at their Gosport yard during the inter-war period.*

contest underlined the success of the NYYC's syndicate-based defence, highlighting the weaknesses inherent in the repeated British challenges made by individual yacht owners.

Nicholson's second J class design *Velsheda*, launched in 1933, was the only J class yacht built for an owner who did not harbour America's Cup ambitions. *Endeavour*, launched the following year, was Sopwith's first America's Cup challenger. Nicholson had played an extensive role in the British adoption of the J class and this helped ensure his unique involvement with the class. He was the only British designer ever to design to this class, and in 1933 the only designer in the world to have had two of his designs for it built. Despite the fact that Nicholson was the obvious choice, Sopwith was also aware that *Shamrock V*'s most significant shortcomings, in comparison with the victorious American yacht *Enterprise*, lay in the area of rig design and construction. To remedy this shortcoming in Nicholson's design ability, from the outset of the *Endeavour* project Sopwith appointed one of his own engineers, Frank Murdoch, to work at Camper & Nicholsons.

Sopwith, the most prominent of the new generation of British owner/skippers, was a marked contrast to Lipton. He managed and skippered his yachts himself and assembled, in addition to the crew, a team of advisors, or afterguard, to assist him. In its objectives this approach was much the same as that employed by Vanderbilt, but in terms of its implementation Sopwith remained essentially an amateur British sportsman challenging the near professional organisation of Vanderbilt and the New York Yacht Club. More specifically Sopwith's poor choice of advisors was largely responsible for his eventual failure, despite the fact that there was virtual unanimity in recognising *Endeavour* as the faster yacht. Even Nicholson's adversary in the 1920 Cup, retired American designer Herreshoff, sought him out personally to acknowledge *Endeavour*'s superiority. Despite having privately predicted '*the inevitable probability of a third defeat*', when this did finally materialise Nicholson was very bitter. Initially he had not intended to travel to America with the challenger, but having gained first-hand insight into the conduct of the race series he publicly blamed Sopwith for

the failure. When he disembarked from the liner *Mauretania* on his return, he pointedly told an awaiting cameraman: '*I have learned for the first time that the fastest yacht does not win the race.*' As if in search of validation for his design from his peer group in America, after the completion of the races Nicholson instigated an exchange of plans with W Starling Burgess, the designer of the winning yacht *Rainbow*. This single act ultimately deprived Nicholson of success in his last attempt at the America's Cup.

Thanks to their use of tank testing, the American designers of the 1937 America's Cup defender *Ranger* were able to analyse the features of *Endeavour* responsible for her speed and incorporate them in the designs. Despite the fact that Nicholson's *Endeavour II* had virtually identical dimensions to *Ranger*'s she was just a stretched *Endeavour*. She showed none of the innovation in hull form that tank testing allowed and *Ranger* outsailed the challenger on every point. Soundly beaten in his final quest for the America's Cup, Nicholson, who had announced on arrival in America that he was getting '*hardened to his fate*', remained

equivocal. True, *Endeavour* (also in America for the Cup) did succeed in becoming the only J class yacht ever to beat *Ranger*, but 1937 was altogether a bad year. In February Nicholson's health had broken down to such an extent that his doctor had advised him to take a holiday abroad, forcing him to miss the launching of *Philante*, the pinnacle of his achievement in motor yacht design. Four months later his wife Lucy died unexpectedly at the age of 64. In America, Nicholson drew solace from his many friends and met the ailing Herreshoff one last time. Despite wanting to see Nicholson, Herreshoff was too ill to leave his bed and when Nicholson called '*they sat together quite quietly and just held each other by the hand*'. From this final encounter with the designer whose achievements he had most sought to emulate Nicholson drew '*tremendous pleasure*'.

Although Herreshoff's yacht design had been based on firm engineering principles, his passing in 1938, combined with the defeats that Nicholson had sustained at the hands of younger, more empirically inclined American yacht designers, marked a threshold in the development of yacht design that Nicholson never crossed. With his designs for the 15 Metre class and for *Shamrock IV* in the years before 1914, Nicholson had been heralded as a designer more inclined to an engineering approach than the then more artistically acknowledged Fife. But Nicholson was unashamedly artistic in his interpretation of his profession and, like Fife, this contributed to his eventual failure. Yacht design and particularly the design of sailing yachts had largely survived in isolation at a time when the use of sail power had been totally eclipsed in other spheres. Although Sopwith partially acknowledged the weaknesses this engendered, he nevertheless also acknowledged Nicholson's genius and sought to compensate for his shortcomings. Others meanwhile embraced the new opportunities offered by technological progress and exploded the hermetisism of yacht design.

The year 1937 marked the end of Nicholson's pursuit of the America's Cup and, as mentioned earlier, Big Class racing had already disappeared in Britain. The death of

LEFT: *An aerial view of Camper & Nicholsons' Southampton yard during the 1930s.*
ABOVE: *The Great Fire of Gosport destroyed the Gosport yard in 1910.*

George V in the previous year reinforced the trend back to the 12 Metre class. Already, in late 1935, Fairey had started the trend by commissioning the 12 Metre *Evaine* from Nicholson and by the end of 1936 the movement had gathered strength, with Nicholson contributing a further four yachts to the class for the 1937 season. Preoccupied with his challenge for the America's Cup, Sopwith did not join the class until 1938, when he acquired the 1937-built, Nicholson-designed *Blue Marlin* (ex-*Alanna*, ex-*Hurricane*). In recognition of Sopwith's exertions in America, Vanderbilt announced his intention to visit Britain in 1939 with a new 12 Metre, *Vim*. The prospect caused a flurry of orders and Nicholson was commissioned to design and build a further two 12 Metres, one of which, *Tomahawk*, was for Sopwith. In a rare move Nicholson took time away from work to helm *Trivia*, his best 1937 12 Metre yacht which her owner had lent him, and was joined on board by his son John. As 1939 headed towards being an '*all round Nicholson season*', with his ocean racer *Bloodhound* winning a notable victory in the Fastnet race, it became apparent that Vanderbilt had another *Ranger* in the Olin Stephens-designed *Vim*. Again Nicholson had not sought to exploit the newly available advantages of tank testing and he suffered the consequences. As in 1914, war soon brushed aside yacht racing but, ironically, whilst the World War I had hindered Nicholson's emergence as the most innovative yacht designer, the interruption of the World War II consolidated Nicholson's reputation by overshadowing yet

another defeat in international yacht racing. At the age of 71, Nicholson's long career in yacht design and construction was nearly over and even he now acknowledged that, '*those days of big yachts will probably not return in our time*'.

During the Second World War Nicholson was extensively involved in converting many of his large motor yachts for wartime use. He adapted some of his motor launch designs for use in air sea rescue work and contributed to the designs of a fast Motor Gun Boat. Much of

ABOVE: *The ketch* Blanche Neige *(now* Aile Blanche*) approaching completion in 1939.*
BELOW: Creole *laid up at Camper & Nicholsons' Southampton yard following her naval service during World War II.*

his Gosport yard was destroyed in bombing raids and this included the bulk of the archives that documented his life's work. With the return of peace Nicholson pinned his hopes for post-war yachting on the smaller classes and waived all his fees for his small boat designs. This strategy was successful, and he received commissions for two dinghy classes: the new 1946 Lee-on-Solent Seagull one design, and the 1947 Fal Estuary restricted class.

Expanding his objectives in 1948, Nicholson sought to stem the increasing popularity of the Norwegian Johan Anker-designed Dragon one design class and replace the now extremely expensive 6 Metre classes with a new less costly small racing yacht class. In 1949 *The Deb* was the first of the new 5.5 Metre class designed to the rule he had first advocated thirty-seven years earlier. Despite such late successes, Nicholson's era was over. His old rival Fife had died in 1944 and the younger designers that had sought to challenge him in the 1930s were taking over. Visiting his yard with declining regularity, he still occasionally enjoyed sailing, and took particular pride in his 1944 election as a Royal Designer for Industry. In 1949 he was awarded the OBE and settled down as the Grand Old Man of yacht design. From 1951 his health gradually declined and he died in February 1954 at the age of 85.

ABOVE: *Laying the deck of J class America's Cup challenger* Shamrock V. LEFT: *The launch of* Shamrock IV, *Sir Thomas Lipton's 1914 challenger for the America's Cup.* HMS Victory *is in the background.*

The Early Yachts

In the 1880s Ben Nicholson was forced to turn to new designers to maintain that part of his business which was dependent on building new yachts. The era in which he had excelled in the design and construction of relatively traditional wooden sailing yachts was over. Nicholson had planned for this in his diversification of the yard away from a reliance on yacht construction. Rather than hold out any hope that his sons might eventually rise to fill the vacant position of in-house yacht designer he simply turned to the new generation of independent designers. The quality of his yard's workmanship was never in doubt and as Nicholson's stranglehold over its production faded so the likes of A Richardson, J Beavor-Webb, G L Watson, C P Clayton, and even a few amateur designers, took up the opportunity of using the yard's facilities. However, the work they generated did not compensate for the loss of an in-house designer. The unexpected emergence of Ben Nicholson's son, Charles E Nicholson as an immensely talented designer led to a new period of design excellence and curtailed the period wherein the Camper & Nicholson yard was substantially reliant on external designers in the decade up to 1890.

Of the independent designers who had yachts built at Camper & Nicholson, Beavor-Webb, with five yachts, was the most significant, despite the fact that none of these was particularly large or indeed significant in the contemporary yacht racing scene. In 1884 when Camper & Nicholson were building *Partridge* to Beavor-Webb's designs, the designer was the focus of international attention since also under construction was *Galatea,* the America's Cup challenger he had designed for Sir Richard Sutton. This more significant yacht was, however, beyond Camper & Nicholson's ability as they did not have the infrastructure to produce the steel frames that the composite structure required. This said, the all wood *Partridge* now remains one of only two Beavor-Webb yachts known still to exist and the only one pre-dating his emigration to the USA. The young Charles Nicholson could hardly have had a richer or more stimulating environment within which to formulate his early ideas.

C E Nicholson's early commissions for yacht designs were almost exclusively for small racing yachts. With these the chances of failure were great: the nature of his lightweight designs called for the highest craftsmanship and the negotiating techniques with which he secured his orders often made them relatively poor business. To compensate, it was essential for Nicholson to build both larger yachts and cruising yachts, where the risks would be smaller and the increased tonnages would be reflected in the profit margins. Still a relative newcomer, C E Nicholson was unable to secure such orders and turned repeatedly during the 1890s to speculative construction so as to give visible proof of what he could accomplish and thus expand his market range. As early as 1890 the yard built the 92 ton TM cruising cutter *Blue Rock,* and whilst this yacht stimulated at least one order for the following year a shortfall for the 1892 season was compensated for by the construction of the cruising cutter *Marigold.* When it came to selling her Nicholson held out for the relatively high price of 1,000 guineas, and several years later still regarded her as one of the best examples of her type.

In her genesis, *Avel* is indebted both to the precedent created by the similarly sized *Marigold* and to Nicholson's enduring French connections. This was the second of three *Avels* that he would design and build for the French yachtsman René Calame. Generously canvassed by today's standards, Nicholson simply described her as 'strong and able'. *Avel* is symbolic of the

success of Nicholson's speculative building in generating commercial orders. However, her relatively small size was a barrier that frustrated Nicholson and this would take him another two years to overcome.

With the commission to design and build *Black Swan*, or *Brynhild* as she was originally named, Nicholson was finally achieving a status that he had felt was all too long in coming; at last he was designing a large yacht. The success of *Brynhild* was one that Nicholson shared directly; as a frequent guest on board he noted that '*we designers do not get any too much practical experience*'. Designed as a cruiser-racer at a time when handicap racing was dominant, *Brynhild* established the basis on which Nicholson would rise from promising newcomer to occupy a leading position in yacht design.

The four yachts shown in this chapter only partially illustrate half of the young Nicholson's design output. Of his early racing yachts, skimming dishes with radical fin and skeg configurations, none survives. Only wood-built, relatively heavy yachts have survived into the twenty-first century, although the stock is far greater than the following pages suggest. Through concerted effort several of the 1896 Bembridge Redwing class have been restored and other candidates for restoration may yet find a future other than gradual decline. By far the most important of these is *Merrymaid*, Nicholson's first great cutter. This 1904, 100 footer remains one of the very few large classics that has yet to be restored and retains a degree of originality both on and below deck that not many restoration projects have benefited from. If *Merrymaid* and, say, one or two other yachts from Nicholson's early career were saved a truly representative collection would be achieved.

Amongst those illustrated there are great disparities. On the one hand, *Partridge*, *Marigold* and *Avel* have all at times been mud-bound with their sailing days seemingly long over. *Black Swan,* on the other hand, has never been out of service. A direct implication of this is that *Black Swan* is now the product of successive alterations; she is no longer yawl rigged as Nicholson intended and her deckhouses have expanded to fulfil the requirements of her successive owners. *Partridge* and *Marigold*'s renewed leases of life came at the eleventh hour. Little remained of either yacht other than distorted but elegant hulls, but in each case a dedicated admirer was found who succeeded in achieving a near archival quality of restoration. For *Avel*, the process was in some ways less remarkable since she had survived virtually intact since being decommissioned in 1928. A large shed over her and a live-aboard custodian ensured preservation through until 1992, when restoration began. The remarkable state of the yacht's preservation combined with sensitive restoration ensured *Avel*'s survival complete with her original interior and as devoid of mechanical and electrical props as she was when Nicholson designed her.

Partridge

Year of build	1885
LOA	22.60m/74ft
LOD	15m/49ft
Beam	3.20m/10ft
Draft	2.60m/8.5ft
Plain sail area	160m²/1722sq ft
Designer	Charles E Nicholson
Builder	Camper & Nicholsons, Gosport

Designed by J Beavor-Webb, *Partridge* was commissioned from the Camper & Nicholson yard by J H Baillie. Built in just five months, the launching ceremony was performed by Miss Nora Lapthorn, daughter of Edwin Lapthorn, the head of the celebrated sailmaking firm. Virtually all the records of *Partridge*'s construction were lost during the successive fires and bombing raids that decimated her builder's records. However, the details of her various owners together with a mid-ship section drawing remain in the archives of Lloyd's Register in London. From the date of her launching up to the present this yacht has had fourteen owners and has seen her name changed to *Rupee* in 1886, *Pollie* in 1889 and *Tanagra* in 1921. As often happened to British yachts whose sailing days were thought to be over, *Partridge* was converted into a houseboat. Further indignities followed, and by 1979 she was lying on her side in the muddy banks of the Blackwater near Tollesbury.

TOP LEFT: *The low profile deck structures sit elegantly beneath an equally low boom.*
BELOW: *The binnacle has been adapted to conceal the engine controls.*
RIGHT: Partridge*'s spectacular rig seen head on as she sails close-hauled ahead of* Avel.

It was only when *Partridge* was rescued by Alex Laird that this yacht's identity and historical importance were established. Laird then began a restoration that lasted twenty years. The work involved replacing all the oak frames, the stem, sternpost and wooden keel, but 95 per cent of the original planking remained sound and was reused. The teak deck, laid out exactly as it would have been at the time, has been reinstated on new deck beams with a plywood sub-deck. The slow pace of the restoration has meant that thousands of hours of careful thought have gone into the process, and this is reflected in all the detail of the restored *Partridge*. Virtually all the work was carried out by Alex Laird as funds and time allowed, making the reborn *Partridge* as much of a testament to his skill as she is to her original builders.

ABOVE: *A light breeze in the bay of St Tropez makes for idyllic sailing.*
RIGHT: *The setting sun lights up a detail of the rigging on board* Partridge *while moored. The blocks are made in teak with bronze frames.*
FOLLOWING DOUBLE PAGE: Partridge *crossing a fleet of modern yachts during the Voiles de St Tropez regatta.*

TOP: *The tiller, lazarette hatch, binnacle and aft skylight. The elegant bronze stanchions give a little extra safety but only in the vicinity of the helm.*

ABOVE: *The outboard end of the main boom: the simple elegant functionality of painted ironwork.*

LEFT: *Copper anti-chafe protects the rail in way of the fairleads.*

RIGHT: *Close-hauled in a fresh breeze* Partridge *dips her leeward rail.*

ABOVE: *In a breeze* Partridge *demands the concentration of all her crew to maintain her racing trim. When cruising, a far smaller crew can handle her.*

TOP RIGHT: *Below decks* Partridge *is stripped out without a bulkhead to interrupt the elegant simplicity of her design.*

CENTRE: *The afternoon sun sets off the warm cotton colour of the material used by sailmakers Ratsey & Lapthorn.*

BELOW: *The neat simplicity of the blocks on the counter.*

FOLLOWING PAGE, LEFT: *Details of* Partridge*'s deck and rig. All the fittings were custom-made, having been researched from contemporary sources. The bronze pieces were cast from specially made patterns and this attention to detail is reflected in the wood and leatherwork.*

FOLLOWING PAGE, RIGHT: Partridge *overhauling* Pen Duick *in a swell off St Tropez with the sirocco blowing.*

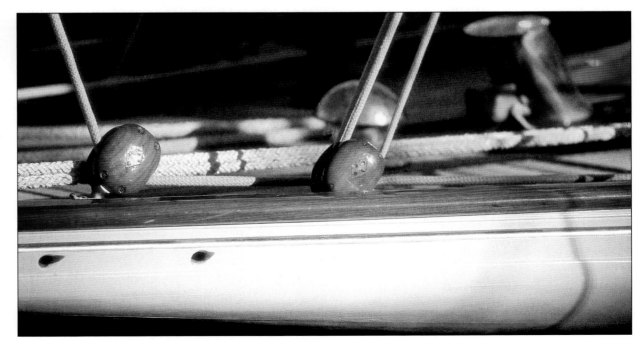

Avel

Year of build	1896
LOD	22.8m/74ft
LWL	13.7m/45ft
Beam	3.8m/12.5ft
Draft	2.3m/7.5ft
Plain sail area	183.4m²/1973ft
Designer	Charles E Nicholson
Builder	Camper & Nicholsons, Gosport

*A*vel was the second of three yachts commissioned from Camper & Nicholsons by the French yachtsman René Calame. Launched on 14 May 1896, her name is Breton for wind. After two years spent cruising with only the occasional race, *Avel* returned to England in the ownership of E W Balne. Her next owner, Arthur C Nicholson (no relation to the yard owners), kept her until 1915 and she subsequently changed hands several times until 1927, when she was decommissioned and turned into a houseboat. To gain extra accommodation, a large deckhouse was built and this greatly helped in her preservation.

In 1990 William Collier mentioned the yacht to Maurizio Gucci, who was immediately charmed by the photographs of her original interior. The restoration was carried out in Cowes under the watchful eye of Harry Spencer. As with *Partridge,* the planking was in remarkably good condition, but the structural timbers required extensive renewal. The interior was carefully removed and refurbished and refitted prior to *Avel*'s relaunch in 1994.

LEFT: *The inboard end of the bowsprit and the base of the mast, together with their miles of associated rigging.*
RIGHT: Avel's *distinctive fiddle bow and slender bowsprit ensure her immediate recognition.*
FOLLOWING DOUBLE PAGE: Avel *on the homeward bound leg during a race at the 1999 Régates Royales in Cannes.*

Of the classic yachts that compete in the Mediterranean regattas, *Avel* is one of the most keenly campaigned. The rig and sail handling gear are faithful to the original design and require a great deal of manual work from the crew, who exhibit great skill and teamwork. Restored as she was built, *Avel* has no engine and the dexterity that is required whilst racing must be maintained as she makes her way back into the harbour.

ABOVE: *The saloon with its original mahogany and pitch pine panelling.*

RIGHT: *The head compartment retains its Victorian hand-painted ceramics.*

OPPOSITE: *At the Régates Royales, Cannes.* Avel *heads towards the finish on the last leg in the clear light typical of westerlies; the wind often freshens in the early afternoon on this leg near the coast. Metre classes as well as classic veteran yachts take part in the Cannes regattas and the 6M class yachts can be seen in the background. During the last week in September 6M, 8M and 12M class yachts race over different courses, filling the bay with sails.*

ABOVE: *A scene during the 1999 Porto Cervo Veteran Boat Rally. The south-easterly wind often comes with a leaden sky and squalls and is always accompanied by a choppy sea. These are not the ideal conditions for a light and agile boat like* Avel; *the waves tend to slow the boat down, especially close-hauled.*

TOP RIGHT: *A detail of the carved scrollwork on the fiddle bow.*

CENTRE: *Sailmaker Mark Ratsey is one of* Avel's *permanent race crew, a role that includes the occasional dunking.*

BELOW: *The saloon seen from starboard. The panelling is set off by the white overhead and leather upholstery. The ornate scrollwork above the panels are of a design typical of Camper & Nicholsons-built yachts of this period, and allows the air to flow behind the panelling.*

LEFT: *A detail of* Avel's *deck with the binnacle at the forward end of the steering cockpit just visible.*

BELOW: Avel *sailing off Cannes alongside the John Alden-designed schooner* Lelantina. *This steel schooner was built in 1929 by Abeking & Rasmussen and although far larger than* Avel *is also far heavier and consequently slower in light conditions. In relative terms* Avel's *rig is far larger, her main boom alone being over 13 metres long.*

OPPOSITE: *A shot against the light of* Avel *running before the wind. Her jib has been lowered and replaced by a large spinnaker.*

Marigold

Year of build	1892
LOD	17.98m/59ft
LWL	14.5m/47.5ft
Beam	3.6m/11.8ft
Draft	2.67m/8.75ft
Designer	Charles E Nicholson
Builder	Camper & Nicholsons, Gosport

There are close parallels in the histories of *Marigold* and *Partridge*. Both are typical Victorian cutters with straight stems and long counter sterns. Equally, both came close to ending their days in mud berths but each found an eleventh hour saviour. What Alex Laird was able to do for *Partridge*, Greg Powlesland did for *Marigold*. Although lacking the funds to undertake the restoration of *Marigold*, Powlesland rescued her and for seven years collected all the archival material he could find. As funds allowed, he consolidated the frail hull until he met Glen Allan, a yachtsman with similar ideas, who was to make the project possible.

TOP LEFT: *The engine controls inside the base of the elegant binnacle.*
BELOW: *A detail of the wood and bronze winch mounted on the mast to hoist the mainsail.*
FACING PAGE, TOP: Marigold *under sail, approaching Plymouth harbour.*
FACING PAGE, BELOW: *A view of the mahogany panelled saloon. Great attention was paid during the restoration to replicate the original joinery techniques.*

The hull was entirely rebuilt by Canal & Marine Services with all new structural members. With the exception of occasional variations in the wood types used, this restoration is amongst the most authentic of all undertaken to date. Where others have opted for plywood sub-decks, *Marigold*'s is traditionally built of teak. Below deck, the rebuilding of the interior benefits from a meticulous attention to detail, down to the horsehair sofas. In line with this, the traditional demarcations have been respected, and whilst the owner's accommodation is lavishly panelled in mahogany, the crew quarters are spartan, with only pine fittings.

ABOVE: Marigold*'s lines epitomise those of the Victorian cutters.*
TOP LEFT: *The mahogany-panelled aft cabin.*
FAR LEFT: *The base of the mast; note the loose-footed mainsail.*
LEFT: *The compaionway that leads to the accommodation below decks, to the side there is a quarter berth for the skipper.*

Black Swan

Year of build	1899
LOA	33.2m/109ft
LWL	25.63m/84ft
Beam	6.10m/20ft
Draft	4.39m/14.4ft
Designer	Charles E Nicholson
Builder	Camper & Nicholsons, Gosport

B*lack Swan* was the result of the first commission Charles Nicholson received for a large yacht. Rigged as a yawl and launched as *Brynhild* in 1899, she became a noted competitor in the handicap racing that dominated British yachting at the time. Changing hands several times in her early years, she was acquired in 1907 by Fredrich Schwann who changed her name to *Black Swann*. Between the wars and in a succession of ownerships she lost her elegant gaff yawl rig and gained an unsightly deckhouse. Amongst the indignities bestowed on her was the new name of *Changrilla*!

I first saw *Black Swan of 1899* as she had been renamed in St Tropez in 1989, and then again in 1991 when she made an appearance at the Porto Cervo Veteran Boat Rally. In 1994 she reappeared in St Tropez but the black topsides that recalled her name had been painted white and with that she had lost a little of her charm but her potential remained. Gradually she has deteriorated and is now in the Beconcini yard in La Spezia, Italy for a thorough overhaul. It can only be hoped that the refit will soon be completed and that she will be restored to her original condition complete with gaff rig.

TOP LEFT: *The steering position.*
BELOW: *The companionway seen from inside the new deckhouse. Originally this yacht was designed as a flush-decked, gaff-rigged yawl.*
OPPOSITE TOP: Black Swan *close-hauled off Porto Cervo in 1991.*
OPPOSITE BELOW: Black Swan *catching both* Altair *and* Orion *on port tack at a race start at the 1994 Nioulargue regatta.*
FOLLOWING DOUBLE PAGE: *The elegance of the hull is clear from this shot taken during the 1991 Porto Cervo Veteran Boat Rally.*

The Cruisers

Until Nicholson was successful in obtaining the commissions to design and build the racing yachts that unequivocally established his position at the forefront of yacht design in the years immediately preceding the First World War, cruising yachts represented the most significant proportion of his output. In the post-war years this trend continued because of the 10-year lapse in large racing yacht construction. Thus, whilst Nicholson can, like most designers, be said to have an undoubted preference for challenges of racing yacht design, commercial realities and his insatiable appetite for large sailing yacht design led him to devote considerable energies to the creation of cruising yachts. In the 1920s when the advent of the motor yacht, for which he was largely responsible, challenged the demand for sailing yachts he successfully developed new types of auxiliaries that ensured continued demand for large cruising sailing yachts.

Built as the ketch *Almara* in 1907, the now schooner-rigged *Joyette* was typical of an enduring type in British yachting. Of all-wood construction and medium proportions, with an easily handled rig, she was intended for an owner who would be actively involved in the management of his yacht and assisted by only a small crew. Despite the radical alterations to the rig, *Joyette* remains highly original on deck and below, the relatively simple joinery is typical of Camper & Nicholsons output. As such, the panelling and other basic features stand direct comparison with those of the schooner *Orion*, but the comparison does not stretch further. Launched as *Sylvana* in 1910, the sheer size of this gaff-rigged schooner puts her in a different category. Dependent on a large crew, this is a yacht that harks back to the very first years of the twentieth century, when schooner building was popular. Unlike *Joyette*, *Orion* always had

auxiliary propulsion but her original paraffin engine provided no more than light assistance in harbour manoeuvres. Although generous by modern standards, her rig was not exceptional amongst comparable cruising schooners. Like all too many vessels intended for world cruising, *Orion*'s career has been confined to Europe, with long periods of ownership in France, Spain and Italy.

Unlike the above yachts, which can by no means be considered cutting edge designs, the 1925 ketch *Sylvia* broke new ground. The use of this rig on such a large yacht was unusual, as was the inclusion of a powerful Gardners diesel engine. Symptomatic of her developmental status was her Bermudan mizzen and gaff main but, like her original black topsides, this sail plan only lasted a year, and by 1926 she was converted to her present rig. A powerful ocean cruiser, *Sylvia* made her maiden voyage, skippered by her owner A S Butler, to Newfoundland, where he married, and the return passage served as honeymoon. Like *Joyette* and *Orion*, *Sylvia* has never suffered the indignities of decommissioning and life in a mud berth, but she came close to meeting her end in the 1980s when an abortive refit in Sardinia led to her being totally dismantled. Thankfully, all the constituent parts were saved and the resultant kit was reassembled in a lengthy refit that was begun in Italy and completed in England. Far from merely saving the yacht, this process ensured that she remained as she was originally, retaining not only her 1926 rig and deck structures but also the most intact interior of any large Camper & Nicholsons-built sailing yacht.

With the advent of Nicholson's design for *Creole*, originally *Vira*, the very large auxiliary sailing yacht was reborn. This was a reinterpretation of a type that had flourished briefly in the 1870s with the incorporation of

steam engines in large sailing yachts. Subsequent advances in steam engines were deemed to make sail redundant and steam yacht evolved as a new branch within yachting. Astonishingly, *Creole*'s genesis stemmed from a request that Nicholson prepare a design for a motor yacht for the American yachtsman Alex S Cochrane. Cochrane had previously commissioned both large sailing and steam yachts but now in his old age wished for a yacht that would not require too large a crew, nor be subject to the vagaries of the wind. Perhaps preying on the sensitivities of a man that commissioned such legendary sailing yachts as the Herreshoff-designed *Westward*, Nicholson convinced Cochrane that his new yacht '*be designed essentially for sailing qualities, but with twin-screw motors to give eleven knots, and so getting near to what I consider a modern auxiliary to be*'.

To overcome the need for a large crew, Nicholson developed a three-masted staysail rig. This was the first time the originally American staysail rig had been adopted by a British designer, and the boldness of its inclusion in the design for a 200 footer left commentators aghast. *Creole*'s early history was overshadowed by Cochrane's increasing infirmity. Worried by the size of the masts, he insisted that these be shortened and Nicholson's masterpiece was mutilated. Others, however, saw the possibilities and orders for the similar three-masters *Ailée* and *Sonia II* soon followed. The unhappy start to *Creole*'s career was characteristic of the ups and downs that were to follow. Under new ownership in 1937 she was restored to the original design, but all too soon her masts were removed again in a wartime conversion. Restored again by Greek shipowner Stavros Niarchos, the 1950s were good to *Creole*, but subsequent service as a school ship left her perilously close to demise. Rescued by the late Maurizio Gucci she is a yacht again,

and though close examination reveals many minor changes from Nicholson's original design her supreme elegance is once more to the fore.

Charles Nicholson's last great cruising yacht, the ketch *Aile Blanche*, originally *Blanche Neige*, is an isolated example at the tail end of his career. Decidedly modern in appearance, her composite construction was typical; her Bermudan rig was by then an accepted standard, but her hull form was a far cry from predecessors such as *Sylvia*. *Aile Blanche* is in many respects an overgrown ocean racer whose antecedents are found in the likes of *Bloodhound*, which also have the stem head rigs that characterise Nicholson's offshore designs of the later 1930s. For all her purist ancestry, this cruising yacht, like *Creole*, had a powerful auxiliary engine, an easily handled rig and was unashamedly modern; the large central deckhouse even included an internal steering position. Delivered to her French owner on the eve of World War II, *Aile Blanche* arrived at her Mediterranean home port just before the outbreak of war. It is rumoured that fear of her confiscation by the occupying troops led to her owner scuttling her for the duration of hostilities. Regardless of this unsubstantiated story, *Aile Blanche* was certainly sailing again by 1948 and looking none the worse. An active career since then has seen her in every ocean of the world, and despite an altered interior and deck structures she remains the practical blue water cruiser that Nicholson had intended.

Orion

Year of build	1910
LOD	39.40m/129ft 3in
LWL	27.42m/90ft
Beam	7.10m/23ft 3in
Draft	4.10m/13ft 6in
Designer	Charles E Nicholson
Builder	Camper & Nicholsons, Gosport

Built in 1910 for Lt Col Courtney Morgan, *Orion* was first christened *Sylvana*. Actively cruised, this yacht changed hands several times and most notably was acquired in 1913 by Count Jean de Polignac, a long-standing admirer of Charles Nicholson's work. In 1921 he sold her to Maurice Bunau Varilla, who renamed her *Pays de France* and based her in Marseille. The following year she returned to England and was acquired by Cecil W P Slade who renamed her *Diane*. In 1927 she passed into the hands of the Argentinian, Raul C Monsegur, who named her *Vira*. Finally, in 1930, she acquired her current name *Orion* when bought by Spaniard Miguel de Pinilios. Throughout her Spanish ownership her home port was Barcelona, where she lay alongside the great Fife schooner *Altair* but unlike that yacht, *Orion* gradually declined.

In 1967 *Orion* lost both masts in the Gulf of Lions and it was not until the 1980s that her new Italian owners restored her sailing condition. Rather than reinstate the original gaff rig, they opted for a staysail rig on the foremast and small gaff mainsail. Under this rig *Orion* was one of the early stalwarts of the Mediterranean classic yacht scene. Over the last decade, as the number of restored classics has grown, *Orion* has shone less bright. With her cut down rig she had neither the power nor the grandeur of her original design.

TOP LEFT: *The binnacle forward of the steering position.*
BELOW: *The mainsheet blocks on the main boom.*
OPPOSITE: Orion *passing* Partridge *at the Régates Royales in Cannes.*
FOLLOWING DOUBLE PAGE: Orion *displaying her power in ideal sailing conditions in the Bay of Cannes in 1999. This followed* Orion's *restoration to gaff rig the preceding year.*

Recently she has been restored to a full gaff rig but still seems to lack a little of the sail acreage she originally set. At the time of her launch, *Orion*'s sails were provided by Ratsey & Lapthorn and she was rigged as a gaff schooner. This classic rig, which was very much in fashion at that time, was developed in the early 18th century along the coast of New England. It was frequently used, particularly by large fishing boats and pilot craft because of its great manoeuvrability and good performance when sailing close to the wind. In Europe the rig reached its height in 1851, when the schooner *America* came to challenge the best English yachts, winning in style and taking home what was to become the America's Cup. With the invention of the Bermudan sail, *Orion* kept her gaff rig on the mainsail, while

between the mainmast and the foremast the new sail plan included a fisherman and staysail. The hull is a composite construction with 80mm (3in) teak planking, mounted on bronze rivets on steel frames; the quick works are covered with copper sheets.

Orion has had an eventful life: in 1935 an explosion and a fire damaged the bridge, wheelhouse and boom, while a storm in the Gulf of Lions broke both masts in 1967. The yacht lay neglected during the 1970s, and by 1978 her state of disrepair was such that she was entrusted to the Beconcini yard in La Spezia, for a thorough restoration, after which she returned in a perfect state. Her original gaff rig has recently been restored.

ABOVE: Orion *gradually catching* Partridge *at the 1999 Régates Royales in Cannes.*

TOP RIGHT AND CENTRE: *Two views of* Orion's *main saloon, which retains its original panelling and fireplace.*

BELOW: *One of the guest cabins.*

TOP: *The bright and welcoming interior of the deckhouse. Guests can enjoy the thrill of the race or cruise in comfort, even in the worst conditions.*

LEFT: *A shot giving some idea of* Orion's *huge sail area.*

ABOVE AND OPPOSITE: *The interior is furnished with antiques; the polished panelling and furniture contrasts with the off-white lining of the deckheads.*

DOUBLE PAGE OVERLEAF: *This action shot of* Orion *and* Saharet of Tyre *neck-and-neck at Porto Cervo in 1989 gives a sense of the sheer speed and power of these yachts.* Saharet of Tyre *was designed in 1933 by Charles Nicholson for American yachtsman Woodbury Parsons.*

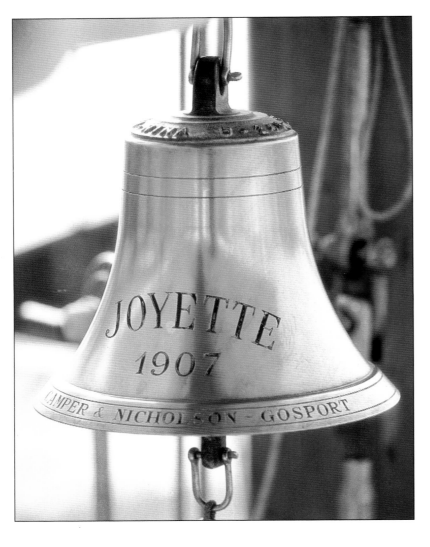

Joyette

Year of build	1907
LOD	27.23m/89ft 3in
LWL	18.89m/62ft
Beam	5.18m/17ft
Draft	3.40m/11ft 2in
Designer	Charles E Nicholson
Builder	Camper & Nicholsons, Gosport

Commissioned by Major H W Calverley and launched in 1907 as the gaff ketch *Almara*, this is a typical cruising yacht of the pre-First World War era. The elegant sheer and low freeboard have led many to look for a racing pedigree in *Joyette*'s ancestry but she was conceived as a cruiser and remained just that. For thirty years she was owned by Sir Osborne Hondell who maintained her as a cruising yacht. It was not until the late 1980s that she found her way to the Mediterranean classic yacht racing circuit, but prior to this *Joyette* underwent extensive changes. She was returned to her original builders for a refit in the mid-1960s, and was thoroughly updated. The elegant counter was cut back, the bowsprit dispensed with and the rig modernised. Fortunately, however, the deck structures and interior survived relatively unscathed. In 1989 *Joyette* emerged from a further refit rigged as a schooner. Whilst she regained many of the attributes expected of classics she remains a far cry from the yacht Charles Nicholson designed.

TOP LEFT: *A close up of the bronze bell.*
BELOW: *A detail of the helm and the binnacle.*
OPPOSITE: Joyette *at the 1992 Imperia regatta; taken into the sun on a misty day, the colour has evaporated*

Under her new schooner rig, *Joyette* has proved that she can be both a fast and a seakindly yacht. The size of the rig however makes her a little less easy to handle than the original ketch rig. Equally, as the organisers of classic yacht regattas become increasingly keen to encourage authentic restoration and institute punitive handicaps on modified yachts, *Joyette* is at a disadvantage on the race course. Laid up now for several years, a further change of ownership may yet see the erroneous schooner rig replaced with the original ketch rig and *Joyette* restored to what she ought to be.

ABOVE: *Another picture taken during the 1992 classic yacht regatta at Imperia; this time the bright light and breeze give* Joyette *the chance to show off her powerful rig.*

TOP RIGHT: *The aft deckhouse is a recent addition but the elegant lines shine through.*

CENTRE: *An old bronze winch which, whilst not original, probably dates back to the pre-Second World War era.*

BELOW: *The main boom end.*

Sylvia

Year of build	1925
LOD	36.88m/121ft
LWL	31.39m/103ft
Beam	7.35m/24ft
Draft	3.99m/13ft
Width	3.99m/13ft
Designer	Charles E Nicholson
Builder	Camper & Nicholsons, Gosport

*S*ylvia's history is inextricably linked to that of Alan S Butler who commissioned her in 1924. An adventurer by nature, he devoted his life to his two passions, flying and yachting. The son of a wealthy English family, he was only 21 years old when he became one of the first Englishmen to own a private plane. Within two years he had commissioned De Havilland to build him another, but this time to his specifications. This order proved vital in assuring the young firm's financial stability, and Butler's involvement with De Havilland deepened until he took over the chairmanship at the age of 25. Two years later he commissioned the stately *Sylvia,* which ranks amongst Charles E Nicholson's largest cruising yacht designs. Immediately after christening his new yacht with his sister's name, Butler set out on a maiden voyage across the Atlantic. Skippering the new yacht himself, he experienced the North Atlantic at its worst before making his landfall in Canada. Ashore he met Lois, his wife to be, and the return passage became their honeymoon.

TOP LEFT: *The steering position retains all its original hardware.*
BELOW: Sylvia*'s original bell mounted on the aft end of the galley deckhouse.*
OPPOSITE: *Bathed in golden light* Sylvia *inches her way out past the island of Phe Phe Le in Thailand.*
FOLLOWING DOUBLE PAGE: Sylvia *in the astonishing Thai landscape.*

Sylvia remains very close to Charles E Nicholson's original design. The teak on steel frame composite hull was restored at the Beconcini yard, whilst the original interior was restored and reinstalled at the Pendennis Shipyard in Falmouth. The most significant changes were made by Butler and Nicholson during *Sylvia*'s first two years. Originally fitted out with a gaff-rigged main, this was converted to the more modern rig on Butler's return from his first transatlantic crossing. Similarly, practicality dictated that the black topsides were soon painted white.

TOP LEFT: *A panoramic shot of the main saloon. The central skylight floods this cabin with natural light and, with the exception of the now removed fireplace, it retains all its original features.*
CENTRE: Sylvia *sailing gently into a tropical sunset.*
BOTTOM: *Lit up by the morning sun the deckhouses are reflected in the newly washed decks.*
ABOVE: *The onset of a tropical storm illustrates the variety of conditions found in the period leading up to the monsoon season.*
OVER LEFT: *Dwarfed by the primeval island,* Sylvia *is both over-shadowed and reflected in the green waters.*
OVER RIGHT: *Dead calm where the heat and mist combine to alter the true colours of the scene.*

Creole

Year of build	1927
LOD	57.97m/190ft 2in
LWL	42.67m/140ft
Beam	9.44m/31ft
Draft	5.35m/15ft 6in
Designer	Charles E Nicholson
Builder	Camper & Nicholsons, Gosport

Charles E Nicholson designed this large, three-masted schooner for the American yachtsman Alexander Smith Cochran, who had previously owned such legendary yachts as the schooner *Westward* and the cutter *Vanitie*. Outstandingly original in concept, *Creole* has joined the pantheon of yachting greats. The staysail rig made all but the foresails self-tacking, but such niceties were not enough for the elderly Cochran, who took fright at the height of the masts and ordered that the rig be cut down. *Creole*, the largest yacht ever built at Camper & Nicholsons' Gosport yard, was thus compromised before she had even set sail.

TOP LEFT: *A close up of* Creole*'s steering position.*

CENTRE: *The central raised steering position, giving the helmsman good all-round visibility, was one of the many innovations Nicholson introduced. A varnished mahogany motor launch is on the right.*

BELOW: *The snug fit-out of the officer's mess with two comfortable leather sofas either side of a reclining drop-leaf table in the forward deckhouse. The radio and navigation instruments can be seen on the far wall.*

OPPOSITE: Creole *under full sail in the bay of St Tropez during a Nioulargue race.*

FOLLOWING DOUBLE PAGE: *A view of the interior of the main deckhouse, with a fine bronze bust in the foreground.*

Inevitably, the now fatally flawed yacht was not a success. An uncomfortable seaboat that could not perform under sail, Cochran soon disposed of *Creole*. In the ownership of Royal Yacht Squadron member Maurice Pope she acquired her legendary name, but it was not until she passed into the ownership of Sir Connop Gutherie in 1937 that *Creole* was finally restored to Nicholson's original designs. *Creole* proved a tantalising sailing yacht, but two short years later her rig was dispensed with as *Creole* passed into the Royal Navy and war service.

ABOVE AND CENTRE: *The owner's suite is panelled in maple inlaid with mahogany and features some of the many antique fittings and paintings that Maurizio Gucci bought for* Creole.
BELOW: *Sail handling on* Creole's *bowsprit as the jib top is lowered at the end of a race.*
OPPOSITE: *In a true sailing breeze,* Creole's *agility under sail comes to the fore, as seen in this shot taken off St Tropez.*

By 1948, *Creole* was in a near derelict condition but still she caught the eye of Greek shipowner Stavros Niarchos, who had her completely restored in Germany. Extravagantly fitted out, *Creole* was Niarchos's private yacht. She ranged throughout the Mediterranean, hosted lavish parties and even participated in the first ever Tall Ships race. Almost overnight Niarchos turned his back on *Creole* and left her dwindling untended in Piraeus. From there she passed into the ownership of a Danish sea school who, though well intentioned, did not have the resources to maintain so large a vessel. As dereliction again loomed for *Creole*, Maurizio Gucci discovered her and developed a passion for this great three-master.

ABOVE: Creole *under sail in a light breeze on a clear autumn day in the Bay of St Tropez. The black hull is set off by the varnished bulwarks and deckhouses.*

RIGHT: *Three different views of the interior of the main deckhouse. Oak and mahogany interweave to create a decorative effect on the floor. The panelling on walls and ceiling is in limed oak. In the centre stands an oval ebony table inlaid with ivory and supported by two unicorns. Marine paintings, antique furnishings and sumptuous sofas all contribute to the refined elegance.*

During the week of the Nioulargue regatta a large tent is set up behind the harbour office in St Tropez to serve as a meeting point where participants can share a beer and discuss the tactics and events during the regatta which has just taken place. I had the good fortune to have a corner of this area to myself for a few years to exhibit my photos.

One evening John Burdon, *Creole*'s skipper, came across from the crowd of yachtsmen with the yacht's owner. After a few jokes and comments about the day's race, I asked Maurizio Gucci's permission to come aboard his yacht to take some photographs and he kindly invited me to visit *Creole* the next morning. At that point someone called me over to ask for some information and I moved away for a few moments. When I turned around I found that Maurizio Gucci had taken on the role of my assistant and was busy persuading a group of yachtsmen to buy my pictures.

ABOVE: Creole *charging along under an ominous sky.*
TOP LEFT: *The two gimbled tables of the dining saloon can be unfolded to form one large dining table. The walls are papered in Japanese ray skin.*
CENTRE: *A desk in the owner's suite matches the ornamental motifs on the walls.*
BELOW: *One of four guest cabins aboard* Creole.

Aile Blanche

Year of build	1939
LOD	30.48m/100ft
LWP	22.78m/74ft 10in
Beam	5.86m/9ft 2in
Draft	3.53m/11ft 7in
Width	6m/19ft 2in
Designer	Charles E Nicholson
Builder	Camper & Nicholsons, Gosport

It was at the 1983 Veteran Boat Rally at Porto Cervo that I first got a close look at *Aile Blanche*. At that time these great classics were only just beginning to be rediscovered by yachtsmen and enthusiasts. Nearly twenty years on, the interest they attract has grown meteorically and classic yacht gatherings are being organised around the world. Bringing yacht owners, sailors and restoration specialists together, these events are now an integral part of an environment that continues to encourage the preservation of this part of our maritime heritage. In 1990 I saw *Aile Blanche* again, this time at the Nioulargue regatta in St Tropez but I did not have the opportunity to go aboard her. I hope to renew my acquaintance with this large ketch before too long.

TOP LEFT: Aile Blanche *close on the heels of the 1929 John Alden-designed ketch* Karenita, *shortly after a start at the 1990 Nioulargue regatta.*

CENTRE: Aile Blanche *in the calmer conditions of Florida Cup day at the 1990 Nioulargue regatta.*

BELOW : *A further view taken at the 1990 Nioulargue regatta.*

OPPOSITE: Aile Blanche *as I first saw her at the 1983 Veteran Boat Rally in Porto Cervo. On the day this shot was taken racing was cancelled on account of strong winds but* Aile Blanche *was among a small number of yachts that ventured out. Here she is seen in the Bay of Pevero.*

The Big Class

The Big Class racing cutters have never ceased to capture the public imagination. From their inception with the construction of *Britannia* in 1893 through to the demise of the J class in 1937, these yachts represented the ultimate in yacht racing in Britain and America. Many were involved in races for the America's Cup but in British waters they were far more important as the premier racing class. As such, the Big Class represented an ideal, but one which frequently proved impossible to sustain. Unduly frequent changes in rating rules were the greatest obstacle to sustained Big Class racing and led the Prince of Wales, later King Edward VIII, to withdraw *Britannia* from racing after just three years. It was the very same problems that prevented C E Nicholson from obtaining a commission to design a Big Class cutter until 1907. In that year a new rating rule, the third since *Britannia*'s construction, was adopted and included many features that Nicholson had long advocated. It paved the way for the Metre classes and the prospect of sustained Big Class racing.

Under the aegis of the first two International Rules of 1907 and 1920, the 23 Metre class was to form the Big Class. The goodwill engendered by the rule led to the amicable resolution of problems caused by the inclusion in the class of older yachts such as *Britannia* and the relatively small Nicholson-designed *Nyria*. With the commission to design the 23 Metre *Brynhild II* in 1907, Nicholson at last had the chance to measure himself against his chief rival William Fife, who designed and built the 23 Metre *White Heather II* and *Shamrock* in 1907 and 1908 respectively. Although *Brynhild* was beset by a series of problems, culminating in her accidental sinking in 1910, it was Nicholson who emerged ahead in the struggle between the two designers. The commission for the America's Cup challenger *Shamrock IV*

followed and Nicholson's pioneering of the Bermudan rig for large racing yachts gained him further advantage in the years following World War I, when the Big Class staggered on with a very mixed fleet.

The first post-World War I commissions for Big Class cutters came in 1928, with Nicholson and Fife securing one apiece. Nicholson's *Astra* was immediately successful, whilst Fife's *Cambria* suffered a number of setbacks, factors that led to Nicholson being commissioned to design *Candida*, another Big Class cutter, in 1929. His dominance over the Big Class achieved, a subsequent rating rule change only served to reinforce Nicholson's position. Complex Anglo-American negotiations led to the British adoption of the American Universal Rule for Big Class racing from 1930 and the replacement of the existing 23 Metre class with the J class. Nicholson was the only British designer who had designed a large cutter to this rule and immediately received the commission to design Sir Thomas Sopwith's last America's Cup Challenger, *Shamrock V*. Subsequently Nicholson was commissioned to design and build three further J class yachts, *Velsheda* in 1933, *Endeavour* in 1934 and *Endeavour II* in 1936.

With the exception of *Endeavour II*, all of Charles Nicholson's inter-war Big Class cutters have survived. By the end of the 1990s all were sailing again but in the intervening years they had fared very differently. With a few modifications *Astra* was able to race against the J class and remained in racing trim after the demise of the class. Briefly sailed in British waters after World War II, *Astra* was sold to Italy in the 1950s, converted into a yawl and finally fell on hard times in the 1980s. In the ownership of Gian Carlo Bussei, *Astra* was rebuilt and sailed again in 1988. Measuring unfavourably under the J class rule, *Candida* was soon withdrawn from racing.

Nicholson himself superintended her 1938 conversion into the cruising yawl, *Norlanda*. Like *Astra* she found a devoted Italian owner and, with the sorry exception of the wholesale replacement of her interior, remained relatively unchanged until rerigged as a cutter in the early 1990s. *Shamrock V* has a similar history; converted for cruising and in Italian ownership under the name *Quadrifoglio*, she returned to Camper & Nicholsons in 1973 for a refit that renewed her structural integrity but took her further away from her racing origins. Acquired by the Museum of Yachting in Newport Rhode Island in 1986, the unsightly high bulwarks and large deckhouse were removed and her original rig reinstated. Since then, *Shamrock V* has changed hands twice and is currently undergoing a refit which will bring her yet closer to her original appearance.

Much of the effort to restore *Astra*, *Candida* and *Shamrock V* to racing trim has been directly inspired by *Velsheda* and *Endeavour*'s remarkable rebirths. Unlike their older sisters, both *Endeavour* and *Velsheda* ceased sailing once their racing days were over. Laid up in mud berths on the British South Coast they attracted little serious attention until the 1980s. True, *Endeavour* had been the target of several amateur attempts to restore her, but none had succeeded. Acquired by Terry Brabant, *Velsheda* was restored and relaunched in 1983. Faithfulness to the original design was limited only by budgetary constraints, of which the relatively light ballast keel and the consequent effect on stability were the most obvious. For nearly ten years *Velsheda* sailed without an engine and with none of the modern sail handling aids that the other restored Big Class cutters have. A change in ownership led to a further refit in which *Velsheda* has undergone radical changes, leaving little original fabric in what had been a uniquely original survivor.

Of all the Big Class restorations, *Endeavour*'s is the most remarkable given how close she lingered at death's door and the extreme state of degradation her hull had reached. Moreover, *Endeavour* was the greatest of Nicholson's Big Class cutters and, in the hearts of sailors, certainly the most beloved of his creations. Supremely beautiful, *Endeavour* was the faster yacht at the 1934 America's Cup and her tantalisingly close shave with victory left Nicholson feeling robbed. In the hands of J class guru Elizabeth Meyer *Endeavour* has won Nicholson a far greater posterity. Relaunched in 1989, *Endeavour* and her tireless owner have been at the core of the reborn Big Class. In September 1989 *Endeavour* and *Shamrock V* raced in the first revival of J class racing in 52 years and since then *Endeavour* has raced against all the other survivors of Nicholson's Big Class.

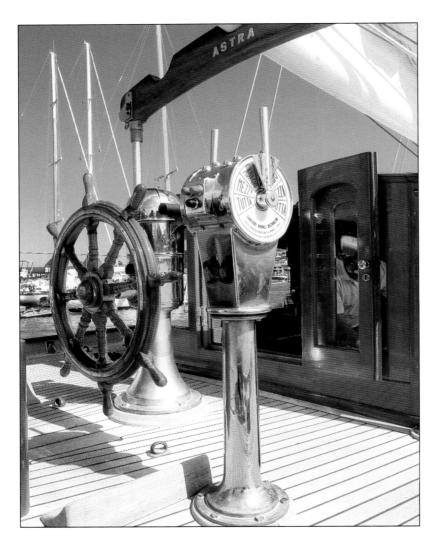

Astra

Year of build	1928
LOD	35.5m/116ft 5in
LWL	22.9m/75ft 1in
Beam	6.2m/20ft 5in
Draft	4.2m/13ft 8in
Plain sail area	665m²/7158sq ft
Designer	Charles E Nicholson
Builder	Camper & Nicholsons, Gosport

After the First World War had brought about the demise of Big Class racing it took ten years of peace for it to be reinstated. Finally, in the autumn of 1927, two new large cutters were commissioned: *Cambria* from William Fife and *Astra* from Charles E Nicholson. *Astra*'s owner was the sewing machine manufacturer Mortimer Singer who, having raced actively in the 12 Metre class, now sought to compete at the sport's pinnacle. Launched on board *Astra*, Singer's initial enthusiasm was not enough to allow him to overcome the pain of injuries sustained in a ballooning accident. Singer took his own life, but *Astra* continued to become one of the most celebrated of the British Big Class cutters.

TOP LEFT: *The steering position remains in its original place but a second deckhouse to contain navigation equipment was added during the 1987 restoration. The engine controls were a further addition.*

CENTRE: *A brass plate in the deckhouse shows the technical specifications and the name of the boatyard in Gosport where* Astra *was built, as well as bearing the name of the Beconcini yard in Italy which restored her in 1987.*

BOTTOM: *Turning blocks for the foresail sheets.*

OPPOSITE: Astra *in a fresh westerly off Porto Cervo.*

FOLLOWING DOUBLE PAGE: *A close up of* Astra *powering along under a large gennaker.*

When *Astra* was acquired by Hugh Paul in 1930 her racing career truly began. Designed under the Second International Rule, *Astra* was slightly smaller than most of her competitors which gave her a significant advantage in handicap racing. When the British adopted the American Universal Rule for Big Class racing in 1930, *Astra* converted particularly well and, unlike *Cambria* and *Candida,* she continued to compete successfully until the demise of Big Class racing in 1936. A light weather flyer, she regularly beat the likes of *Shamrock, Endeavour, Britannia* and the schooner *Westward.* When the Big Class was disbanded, Hugh Paul continued to sail *Astra,* using her as mother ship to a new 12 Metre he called *Little Astra.* Like so many first class British racing yachts after the war, *Astra* headed

for the Mediterranean, where she survived as a cruising yacht prior to being restored.

ABOVE: Astra *close-hauled in a light breeze with the island of Caprera in the background.*
TOP RIGHT: Astra's *interior is panelled in light oak; shown here is a view of the main saloon.*
CENTRE AND BELOW: *Views of two guest cabins.*
FOLLOWING DOUBLE PAGE: Astra *seen bow-on during the 1995 Veteran Boat Rally in Porto Cervo.*

Candida

Year of build	1929
LOD	35.7m/117ft
LWL	24.2m/79ft 5in
Beam	6.3m/20ft 7in
Draft	4.8m/15ft 8in
Plain sail area	760m²/8180sq ft
Designer	Charles E Nicholson
Builder	Camper & Nicholsons, Gosport

Designed by Charles Nicholson a year after *Astra*, *Candida* was also designed under the Second International Rule. However, the philosophy behind this yacht was very different; she is an altogether larger yacht, designed to perform in heavier conditions. Her owner, British banker Herman Andrea, hoped that with such a powerful yacht he would be able to dominate the racing scene. However, *Candida* was generally not able to achieve the speeds required for her to win under the handicapping system in use at the time. With the adoption of the Universal Rule by the British in 1930, *Candida*'s problems were compounded; she did not measure well under that rule and could claim virtually no allowance from the faster J class yachts. A keen helmsman, Andrea sought to update *Candida* at every opportunity, but eventually gave up the unequal struggle against the rule and bought the J class yacht *Endeavour* from Sir Thomas Sopwith.

TOP LEFT: *The original wheel mounted on deck. Like all the Big Class cutters the helmsman stood on deck with no protection from the elements.*

BELOW: Candida's *elegant counter. The two mainsheet winches are relatively recent additions.*

OPPOSITE: Candida *sailing with a reefed mainsail under a threatening sky in St Tropez in 1993.*

FOLLOWING DOUBLE PAGE: *Heeling to a gust* Candida *dips her lee rail.*

Off the racing circuit, *Candida* was converted for cruising at Camper & Nicholsons' yard. A yawl rig replaced the towering single spar, the lead keel was trimmed, and a larger deckhouse was fitted. Rechristened *Norlanda* and based in the Mediterranean, *Candida*'s owner was so inspired by the restorations of *Astra* and *Endeavour* that he converted his yacht back to her original specifications. In 1991, after a substantial refit at the Beconcini yard, *Candida* emerged looking much as she had done in 1929. Since then she has raced again with *Astra* and *Endeavour*.

ABOVE: Candida *crewed by the* Corum *sailing team awaiting the beginning of the starting sequence for a race at the 1993 Nioulargue regatta off St Tropez.*

TOP RIGHT: *Threatening clouds during a Florida Cup race against* Agneta *at the 1995 Nioulargue regatta.*

CENTRE: *A view of the saloon.*

BELOW: *A trompe l'oeil bookcase in the saloon.*

FOLLOWING DOUBLE PAGE: Candida *entering the harbour of St Tropez after a day's racing. The three-masted schooner* Adix *can be seen in the background.*

Shamrock V

Year of build	1930
LOD	36.6m/120ft
LWL	24.7m/81ft
Beam	6m/19ft 8in
Draft	4.5m/14ft 9in
Plain sail area	699m²/7524sq ft
Designer	Charles E Nicholson
Builder	Camper & Nicholsons, Gosport

In 1929 Sir Thomas Lipton made his fifth and final challenge for the America's Cup but only succeeded in consolidating his title as the world's best loser. The American defender *Enterprise* was technically far more advanced than *Shamrock V* but, more important, was campaigned by Harold Vanderbilt with greater professionalism than the ailing Lipton was able to bring to his challenge. Although it was too late for Lipton, *Shamrock V* helped the British raise their game. After Sir Thomas Lipton's death, *Shamrock V* was acquired by Sir Thomas Sopwith, who used her as a test bed for the superlative *Endeavour*. In 1934, and now known simply as *Shamrock*, she passed into the hands of Sir Richard Fairey, who maintained her as one of the stalwarts of the inter-war Big Class.

TOP LEFT: *Shamrock V's original wheel has been extended with the addition of an extra external hoop.*
BELOW: *A close up of the binnacle.*
OPPOSITE: *An aerial view of* Shamrock V *at the 1999 Antigua Classic Yacht Regatta. With gusts touching 40 knots the seventy-year-old Cup challenger provided some unforgettable moments for those on board.*
FOLLOWING DOUBLE PAGE: *The 1999 Antigua Classic Yacht regatta closed a phase in* Shamrock V's *life in grand style. Her new owner elected to send her to the Pendennis Shipyard for a further restoration that will bring her closer to Charles Nicholson's original designs.*

Unlike the other British J class yachts, *Shamrock V* has never been out of commission. Like *Astra* and *Candida*, she found a new life in the Mediterranean, and when age took too great a toll she was returned to Camper & Nicholsons' yard and completely rebuilt. The yacht that emerged from this refit had regained structural integrity but differed greatly from Nicholson's designs. New waist-high bulwarks had been added, as had a full height deckhouse. The rig, however, had been shortened and, whilst for a time she remained the only J class in commission, she bore little resemblance to the beauty of the 1930s. In the late 1980s *Shamrock V* passed into the ownership of the Newport-based Museum of Yachting where, under the guidance of Elizabeth Meyer, she was gradually improved. Now back in private ownership she is undergoing the major refit that will see her emerge yet closer to the original designs.

LEFT (IN ORDER FROM THE TOP): *A view of the saloon with maple panelling installed for the Italian Mario Crespi, the owner of* Shamrock V *just after the Second World War; in the aft cabin maple is combined with mahogany to create decorative effects; a view of the bathroom with the hand-painted porcelain washbasin; one of the guest cabins, also with panelling and furniture in maple. In contrast to the other J class yachts,* Shamrock V, *had several owners over the years and was never completely abandoned. This ensured that she was always kept in sailing condition and has preserved her original rig to the present. Even the yellow pine deck is original.*

OPPOSITE: *During the 1999 Antigua regatta the sea and wind put the strength of the hull and rig to the test. On this occasion* Shamrock V, *the only J class yacht built using wooden planking, shows she can stand the worst that the sea can throw at her.*

DOUBLE PAGE OVERLEAF: Shamrock V *and* Velsheda *jockeying for position during pre-start manoeuvres.*

Velsheda

Year of build	1933
LOD	38.8m/127ft
LWL	25.4m/83ft
Beam	6.5m/21ft
Draft	4.6m/15ft
Plain sale area	706m²/7600sq ft
Designer	Charles E Nicholson
Builder	Camper & Nicholsons, Gosport

Commissioned by Woolworths chairman William F Stephenson, *Velsheda* was launched in 1933 and named after his three daughters Velma, Sheila and Daphne. When Stephenson took up yachting he bought the 1907 Fife-designed cutter *White Heather II* but, finding that no amount of improvements could truly make her competitive, she was scrapped at the end of the 1932 season. The old cutter's lead keel was melted down for reuse in the construction of the first all steel British J class which was to be a state of the art racing yacht. In *Velsheda*'s hull structure Camper & Nicholsons pioneered many construction techniques subsequently used in the hulls of *Endeavour* and *Endeavour II*. Though Stephenson harboured no ambitions to challenge for the America's Cup, his support for the J class paved the way for Sir Thomas Lipton's two challenges and helped ensure that the British Big Class remained at the forefront of technical developments.

TOP LEFT: *A close up of* Velsheda's *new wheel and binnacle set in the cockpit which was installed during the last rebuild.*
BELOW: *The crew hatch forward of the mast.*
OPPOSITE: *A bird's eye view of* Velsheda *flying a gennaker.*

Stephenson was the last of the older breed of British yachtsmen. Unlike his contemporaries such as Sopwith, Paul and Andrea, he remained relatively aloof from racing and employed a professional helmsman. This, however, was no reflection of his enthusiasm, and he campaigned *Velsheda* actively at all the British regattas until the class broke up in 1936. Her racing career over, *Velsheda* was laid up in a mud berth on the Hamble, where she served as a houseboat until acquired by Terry Brabant in the early 1980s. Brabant restored *Velsheda* simply: on deck she remained very similar to how she had first appeared, below she had neither engine nor any other of the complex systems that all the surviving J class now have. *Velsheda* was the first of the J class to be restored to her original rig and did much to inspire the rebirth of the Big Class.

TOP LEFT: *An example of the fine joinery aboard the rebuilt* Velsheda.
BELOW LEFT: *A view of the saloon with mahogany panelling; the table is decorated with inlaid wood.*
BELOW RIGHT: *The saloon seen from a different angle, with sofas and an inlaid occasional table with a globe set in the centre.*
ABOVE: *A beautiful image of* Velsheda *in weather conditions typical of the Antigua regattas.*

In 1992 *Velsheda* changed hands but an ambitious refit soon ran into problems. After a further change of ownership, a complete rebuild was undertaken at Southampton Yacht Services with Gerard Dijkstra in charge of naval architecture and John Mumford in charge of interior design. The new *Velsheda* that emerged in 1996 is no longer a stripped out low-tech racer, and now includes all the amenities associated with a modern yacht. To achieve this the original design was compromised in certain areas. Like *Astra*, *Velsheda* acquired a second deckhouse and was fitted out for world cruising. Reunited with the two other surviving J class yachts at the 1999 Antigua regatta, *Velsheda* proved fastest round the course but was unable to save her time within the handicap system under which these yachts now race.

ABOVE: Velsheda *at the 1998 Antigua Classic Week exhibiting a flawless paint finish.*

TOP RIGHT: *The mainsheet track.*

CENTRE: *A bird's eye view of* Velsheda's *bow; note the lone bowman calling the trim of the foresails.*

BELOW: *A plethora of halyards at the mast base.*

FOLLOWING DOUBLE PAGE: *At the 1999 Antigua Classic Yacht regatta the three surviving J class yachts raced together for the first time since the 1930s.*

Endeavour

Year of build	1934
LOD	39.6m/130ft
LWL	26.5m/87ft
Beam	6.7m/22ft
Draft	4.6m/15ft
Plain sail area	557m²/5996sq ft
Designer	Charles E Nicholson
Builder	Camper & Nicholsons, Gosport

When Sir Thomas Sopwith elected to challenge for the America's Cup, he naturally turned to Charles Nicholson, who had provided him with his celebrated 12 Metre *Mouette*, and who was then established at the apex of British yacht design. Sopwith's approach was methodical and he sought to give his new yacht the benefits of his aeronautical expertise. To achieve this, he delegated aeronautical engineer Frank Murdoch to work full time at the Gosport yard and bought *Shamrock V* to gain real performance data. In genesis *Endeavour* had every advantage and her unsurpassed beauty captured the public's imagination. A last minute change from a professional to an amateur crew just before the America's Cup races was widely blamed for *Endeavour*'s failure to capture that elusive trophy, but in reality it was tactical errors and the weakness of the Sopwith afterguard which were responsible. The best of all the British J class yachts, *Endeavour* acquired a legendary status which was only increased by her descent into a derelict condition and her subsequent eleventh hour rescue.

TOP LEFT: Endeavour*'s new wheel following the 1989 restoration.*
BELOW: *Modern winches make it possible to sail with a fraction of the original crew.*
OPPOSITE: Endeavour *battling it out with* Velsheda *off Antigua.*
FOLLOWING DOUBLE PAGE: *A spectacular helicopter shot; there are 40 people on deck.*

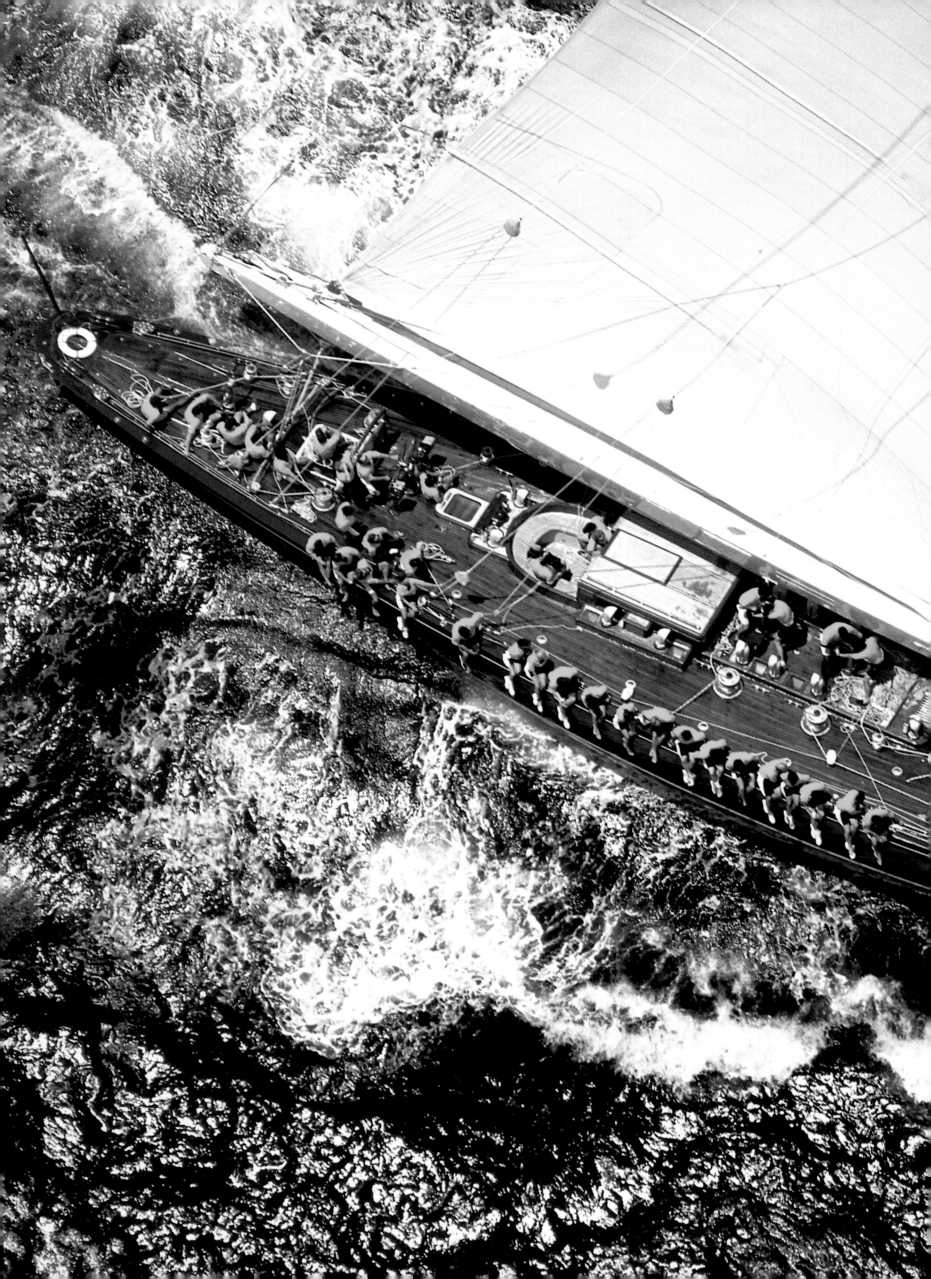

Endeavour dominated the British Big Class throughout the remaining years of J class racing. In 1935 she and the American visitor *Yankee*, remained closely matched. In 1936 she acted as trial horse for *Endeavour II* and commentators remained split as to which was the faster yacht. Endeavour returned to Newport with Sopwith's new challenger *Endeavour II* in 1937. During the New York Yacht Club cruise that followed the Cup races *Endeavour* became the only yacht ever to beat the legendary J class *Ranger*, which had so easily put an end to Sir Thomas Sopwith's second challenge. This, however, was her last outing before being condemned to a mud berth. Various efforts to save *Endeavour* had failed prior to the intervention of Elizabeth Meyer. Faced with a hull that was too weak to be moved, Meyer

built a yard where the hull lay at Calshot Spit on the Solent. When the steelwork was complete the hull was relaunched and towed to the Royal Huisman Shipyard in Holland, where all the remaining work was undertaken. When *Endeavour* was recommissioned in 1989 she sailed to Newport Rhode Island and raced *Shamrock V* in the first series of J class races to be held in 62 years.

TOP LEFT: Endeavour*'s interior is panelled in cherrywood. These two views show the main saloon, complete with working fireplace. To starboard is* Ranger*'s transom, a reminder that* Endeavour *was the only J class ever to beat the 1937 Cup defender.*

BELOW: *The owner's cabin, which has an en suite bathroom, and one of the smaller guest cabins.* Endeavour *can accommodate an owner's party of eight.*

ABOVE: *With her spinnaker set in a 30 knot breeze* Endeavour *is hauled bodily through the water.*

FOLLOWING DOUBLE PAGE: *The forward third of* Endeavour*'s hull has risen out of the sea as she rides the Atlantic swell.*

The Ocean Racers

The emergence of ocean racing in the mid-1920s was one of the first genuinely new developments in British yacht racing for many years. This new branch of the sport had originated in America and in its early years in Britain was both controversial and of minority interest. With the founding of the Fastnet race in 1925, the sport's British supporters established a new forum for international competition but, whilst they rallied home grown participants who set off in a mixed fleet of old cruisers and converted workboats, they were at a great disadvantage compared to the Americans, who had given the subject far greater attention and had already developed purpose-designed offshore racing yachts.

Nicholson's attraction to ocean racing was based on a large number of factors, and not just patriotic motivation. Viewing himself as the foremost British designer, it was important to him that he be involved in all aspects of yachting. To achieve this he was willing to spend a disproportionate amount of energy on what in business terms was barely worthy of his consideration. Of particular relevance to his interest in early ocean racing was that the rating rule adopted was a variant of one he had unsuccessfully promoted many years earlier; it encouraged genuinely seaworthy racing yachts of a type that met with Nicholson's wholehearted approval. Added to these factors was the undoubted pleasure that Nicholson took from the successful participation in the Fastnet of the yachts *Gull* and *Ilex,* which he had designed back in 1896 and 1899 respectively.

Although Nicholson never participated in the Fastnet himself, when the race appeared to lack support in 1933, he entered his own yacht *Flame* to help make up numbers. Two years later the first of his four ocean racers was launched for Isaac Bell, an American yachtsman

resident in Britain, and with this first opportunity to design an ocean racer Nicholson sought finally to brush aside all the criticism of the new sport. First he had to persuade Bell that he would not willingly enter into a collaboration with leading American designer Olin Stephens and, this successfully achieved, he set out to design a yacht that would conform not only to the ocean racing rule but also to the 12 Metre class of the International Rule. In doing this, Nicholson succeeded in producing an admirable ocean racer and also challenged those who had criticised the new sport. Typically these were the advocates of inshore racing who demanded far more extreme yachts, such as the pure 12 Metres, which were not nearly as seaworthy and offered no use other than out and out racing. With *Foxhound* Nicholson created a yacht that with '*a little loss in smooth water weatherliness, compared with a 12 Metre, gained the oceans of the world*'. This ended all criticisms of ocean racing by highlighting the shortcomings of the long-established racing types.

The success of *Foxhound* was such that her owner received an offer he could not refuse at the end of her first season. An unwilling seller, Bell immediately returned to Nicholson and commissioned the construction of the near sister *Bloodhound* for the 1936 season. Having proved his point with *Foxhound*, Nicholson could scarcely continue to maintain his refusal to collaborate with Olin Stephens who was to be partially responsible for *Bloodhound*'s rig in a unique collaboration that has remained largely unacknowledged. Nicholson's sustained enthusiasm for the type led him to start the speculative construction of the third and final of his 12 Metre ocean racers in late 1936. Prior to launching in 1937, *Stiarna* had been acquired by Lieut J F B Gage, and although a successful yacht she was

never campaigned with the same vigour as her two predecessors.

Nicholson's fourth and final ocean racer *Firebird X*, now *Oiseau de Feu*, was a totally new design launched in 1937. Larger than her predecessors, she was one of the first yachts to show the influence of the next generation of Nicholsons, namely C E Nicholson's nephew Charles A Nicholson. Undoubtedly Charles E Nicholson was responsible for the lines, sail plan and general characteristics but, unlike her ocean racing predecessors, *Oiseau de Feu* was built at Camper & Nicholsons' Southampton yard, where Charles A Nicholson had just launched his first major design, the 1936 ocean racer *Yeoman*. The young Nicholson was just one of many relatively new yacht designers focusing on ocean racing and, whilst he only achieved major recognition post-World War II, when his second *Yeoman* won the 1951 Fastnet outright, at the time of *Oiseau de Feu*'s construction, he was already exercising influence on the detailed design of the deck structures and the minutiae of the deck layout.

All the Nicholson ocean racers had extraordinarily long racing careers and remained relatively unchallenged in the face of increasingly light displacement competitors through to the 1960s. *Bloodhound*'s exceptional string of pre-war victories set her apart from her stable-mates, a factor which was further emphasised post-war when her acquisition by the Queen and Duke of Edinburgh cast her firmly in the limelight. Since this high profile ownership she has suffered vagaries of fortune, but recent refits have seen her sailing again, ever the able and fast all rounder that Nicholson intended. At present the fate of *Foxhound* is unknown; actively campaigned by Portuguese owners in the 1960s, the first of Nicholson's legendary trio has since seemingly disappeared. *Stiarna* suffered various indignities but after a long period laid up in Florida was bought by an owner intent on restoring her in New England. Tragically, whilst on passage from the Caribbean in early 1999, fire broke out aboard forcing her crew to abandon her at sea. *Oiseau de Feu*, long in French ownership, has benefited from a major rebuild which, although not restoring her original cutter rig, it has ensured that, as with *Bloodhound* she remains an actively raced yacht.

Bloodhound

Year of build	1936
LOD	19.26m/63ft 2in
LWL	13.72m/45ft
Beam	3.81m/12ft 6 in
Draft	2.77m/9ft
Designer	Charles E Nicholson
Builder	Camper & Nicholsons, Gosport

The second of three very similar ocean racers designed by Charles E Nicholson, *Bloodhound* has enjoyed a glittering career. She succeeded the acclaimed *Foxhound*, was actively campaigned by Isaac Bell, and established an enviable pre-war racing record that culminated in victory in the 1939 Fastnet race. Post-war, *Bloodhound* was closely associated with the British royal family, by whom she was acquired. The Duke of Edinburgh campaigned her actively and she was also used for family sailing. This long career as both a racing and cruising yacht testifies to the genius of her designer's original intent. *Bloodhound* successfully combines many of the attributes of the more delicate 12 Metre class yacht with the more rugged characteristics that allow her to perform well offshore.

TOP LEFT: *A modern wheel has replaced the more traditional original one.*

BELOW: *The rounded deckhouse is one of the features that makes* Bloodhound *instantly recognisable.*

OPPOSITE: *Under sail on the Solent,* Bloodhound's *design antecedents in the 12 Metre class are clearly visible.*

Bloodhound's original rig was designed by Olin Stephens in a rare Anglo-American collaboration. Today the original wooden spars have been replaced with an alloy rig designed by Illingworth & Primrose. An extremely practical yacht, *Bloodhound* has never ventured to the Mediterranean classic yacht gatherings but can often be seen plying her home waters on the Solent.

TOP LEFT: *The main deckhouse seen from another angle.*
CENTRE: *A picture of* Bloodhound *taken during the Hermès Mumm Trophy at Cowes in 1998. With 35 knots of wind, she is sailing comfortably with a jib, foresail and mainsail without reefs.*
BELOW: *The teak hatch leading to the crew's quarters forward of the main mast.*
ABOVE: *Close-hauled off Cowes,* Bloodhound *powers down the Solent.*

Oiseau de Feu

Year of build	1937
LOD	20.72m/68ft
LWL	14.72m/48ft 4in
Beam	3.96m/13ft
Draft	2.96m/9ft 8in
Designer	Charles E Nicholson
Builder	Camper & Nicholsons, Gosport

O*iseau de Feu* was the last of the four ocean racers designed by Charles E Nicholson during the inter-war period. By 1937, when she was launched, Big Class racing in Britain had died out and yachtsmen were even keener to experiment with new types. Commissioned by Ralph Hawkes and originally named *Firebird X*, *Oiseau de Feu* illustrates a turning point in Charles E Nicholson's career. In his late sixties, the famous designer was very slowly beginning to let the reins of power slip from his hands. Unlike other sailing yachts of comparable size, *Oiseau de Feu* was built at the firm's Southampton yard, which usually built larger steel yachts. In Southampton Nicholson's nephew Charles A Nicholson was just beginning to establish a reputation and exerted considerable influence over the finer points of this yacht's design, the lightweight cedar deck structures being the most obvious example.

TOP LEFT: *A close up of the wooden wheel.*

CENTRE: *Originally the deck structures were built in cedar and to a design that varied from Camper & Nicholsons' standard practice; this was faithfully replicated during the restoration.*

BELOW: *The cockpit complete with some additional winches.*

OPPOSITE TOP: *Close-hauled off St Tropez at the 1995 Nioulargue regatta.*

OPPOSITE BELOW: *A view of the saloon. The restoration was carried out by the Raymond Labbé yard in St Malo to a design by Guy Ribadeau Dumas.*

Firebird X did not achieve her full racing potential in the pre-war years, but with the return of peace and under the ownership of Hugh Crankshaw became far better known. Several rig changes were experimented with, including the addition of a bowsprit, and in the 1950s she was a stalwart of the ocean racing scene. In 1962 a change of ownership took her to France, where she has remained ever since. She was first renamed *Flamme II* and then in 1970 *Vindilis II*. She reverted to the French eqivalent of her original name in 1983. Since then a major rebuild has been carried out by the Labbé yard in St Malo. The interior layout has slightly altered but retains its period charm.

TOP LEFT: *A detail of the chrome-plated binnacle complete with removable compass light. This American pattern fitting is probably not the original.*
CENTRE: *The companionway and a corner of the saloon; note the folding basin.*
BELOW: *The forward cabin now occupies an area that was originally given over to the paid crew..*
ABOVE: Oiseau de Feu *off the Lerin Islands whilst competing in the Régates Royales at Cannes in 1999, by then cutter-rigged again.*

The Twelve Metres

As with the Big Class, it was the introduction of the International rule in 1907 that provided the background of stability against which Charles E Nicholson was to excel. Initially, the 12 Metre class was not of great significance. British yacht racing had long had an intermediate size class; under the rule that preceded the introduction of the Metres classes it had been the 52 foot Linear Raters, and Nicholson's performance in that class had been nothing but chequered. Under the new rule, the 15 Metre class took over from the 52 footers and his previously less than successful yachts haunted Nicholson until he obtained the commission for *Istria* in 1912. The relatively low profile 12 Metre class was initially pioneered in Scotland under the aegis of designers T C Glen-Coats and William Fife and sailed mainly on the Clyde. From Scotland it spread not to the British south coast but to Argentina, where the class was taken up by the Yacht Club Argentino and later gained popularity in Scandinavian countries. It was only in the aftermath of World War I, when the 15 Metre class was not resurrected, that 12 Metres became the prime intermediate size yachts in British racing. From 1927 onwards, when the class was adopted in the USA, it finally assumed the status that would lead to it being chosen for the America's Cup post-World War II.

Consistent with this, Nicholson's first 12 Metre, *Rafaga,* was built for export to Argentina in 1908. In 1914 he designed *Skum III*, which was built in Sweden, but it was not until 1924 that he would design another 12 Metre. The post-World War I revival of the 12 Metre class was spearheaded by Fife's 1923 *Vanity,* and Charles E Nicholson's *Clymene* was his first contender in a class where Fife was still thought to be the more dependable designer. Nicholson contributed *Doris* to the class in 1925 and two years later was commissioned by Sir

William Burton to design and build *Iyruna* whose name, standing for International Yacht Racing Union with North America, celebrated the class's now brighter horizons. Despite Nicholson's highly successful *Mouette*, built for Sir Thomas Sopwith in 1928, and the equally promising *Flica*, for Sir Richard Fairey of the following year, the class did not continue to grow. Instead the leading 12 Metre owners graduated to the Big Class. But whilst this temporarily halted the growth of the 12 Metre class it also contributed to Nicholson's dominant position. When the Big Class ceased racing after 1936, Nicholson's stranglehold was transferred from it to the 12 Metres. Thus, whilst Fife secured more orders in the earlier years of the inter-war period, it was Nicholson who eventually prevailed, with thirteen yachts versus Fife's eleven. Playing second fiddle to these two big name designers was Mylne, with four commissions throughout the period, and finally Jack Laurent Giles whose sole contribution, the 1939 *Flica II,* was to have far greater influence post-World war II than during Nicholson's career.

Having designed to the 12 Metre class since its inception, C E Nicholson's 12 Metres reflect the evolution of the class as well as the impact of the 1920 and 1934 revisions of the International Rule. Sadly there is no evidence to believe that either of his pre-World War I designs survive. The inter-war designs have fared far better; *Clymene*, the first, survives and though variously modified has now been classed as a national monument in France and is currently undergoing a total restoration. Sir Thomas Sopwith's legendary 1928 *Mouette* was sold to America in the 1930s and sadly does not survive. The very similar and comparably successful 1929 *Flica,* originally built for Sopwith's sporting and business rival Sir Richard Fairey, has long been out of

commission but survives and is awaiting restoration; an outstandingly worthy candidate.

The sheer number of yachts built following the 1934 revision of the rating rule has led to a significant survival rate. Wartime losses include the 1934-built *Westra*, *Blue Marlin* (ex-*Alanna* and *Hurricane*) of 1937 and the 1939 *Ornsay*. The 1937 *Little Astra* survived in the Mediterranean until the 1960s before disappearing, but the others have survived. Some have been the subject of implausibly wide ranging restorations, when their deteriorated conditions necessitated the replacement of nearly all their fabric. Most significant in this category is the 1939 *Tomahawk*, Nicholson's ultimate 12 Metre. Acquired by Fiat boss Gianni Agnelli in the 1950s, *Tomahawk* was well known in Italian waters, but when rediscovered in the mid-1980s by her current owner only the frail shape of the former beauty remained. The reconstruction saved the yacht but she is a far cry from the 1939 design. *Trivia*, one of the four 1937 Nicholson-designed 12 Metre yachts, had a long career. In the 1950s, as *Norsaga*, she was used for research for the eventually abortive Red Duster Syndicate's America's Cup challenge. In a series of disasters, she sank in America during the 1970s, was acquired for restoration and shipped back to Britain in the mid-1980s only to be dropped on arrival. Finally, a further change in ownership ensured that she was restored back at the yard where she had originally been built.

There are two other survivors from Nicholson's mid-1930s 12 Metre designs. Most significant is the 1936 *Evaine*, built for Sir Richard Fairey, an extremely successful yacht which was campaigned through the 1950s including a 1958 role as trial horse for *Sceptre*, the first of the 12 Metre challengers for the America's Cup. Although *Evaine* has not sailed for a few years she survives in largely sound condition with her 1950s aluminium rig. *Aile*, formerly *Wings*, built in 1937 is a final survivor and though equal in elegance to her sisters this was the one 12 Metre that never raced and consequently remains a little less interesting.

Despite the relatively high survival rate of Charles Nicholson's 12 Metres, none retains the full integrity of his original design. The stock of yachts and available archival data would allow a restoration that would reveal the beauty of Nicholson's 12 Metre designs in all their original simplicity.

Clymene

Year of build	1924
LOD	20.48m/67ft
LWL	13.78m/45ft 3in
Beam	3.72m/12ft 3in
Draft	2.70m/8ft 9in
Designer	Charles E Nicholson
Builder	Camper & Nicholsons, Gosport

Built at Camper & Nicholsons' Gosport yard in 1924, *Clymene* is the oldest Charles E Nicholson-designed 12 Metre yacht that survives. Commissioned by London-based advertising agent Peter de G Benson *Clymene* was one of the yachts that spearheaded the post-First World War development of the 12 Metre class. With the modification of the International Rule in 1934 she was superseded within her class but continued to race actively. During the later 1930s she sailed as both *Moyana IV* and *Alkor II*, and, rigged as a yawl, took on the celebrated ocean racers of that era. When raced at the 1990 Nioulargue regatta and Régates Royales, *Clymene* was clearly in need of major work. Today she has been declared a national monument in France and a total rebuild is underway in Bandol.

TOP LEFT: *Under spinnaker in the Bay of St Tropez.*
BELOW: *Two recent pictures showing the partly restored hull with some new framing.*
OPPOSITE: *Under sail prior to starting the restoration which, if completed to the original designs, will reveal* Clymene *as a real thoroughbred.*

Trivia

Year of build	1937
LOD	21.33m/70ft
LWL	13.99m/45ft 10in
Beam	3.59m/11ft 8in
Draft	2.79m/9ft
Designer	Charles E Nicholson
Builder	Camper & Nicholsons, Gosport

Built for shipowner, V W MacAndrew, *Trivia* was amongst the best 12 Metres that Charles Nicholson ever designed. She dominated the 12 Metre class in her first season, and has only rarely stopped racing since. In the 1939 season, which was dominated by *Vim* and *Tomahawk*, *Trivia* was loaned to Nicholson, who campaigned her himself. Post-war and renamed *Norsaga*, *Trivia* was based in Norway before returning to Britain where she was skippered by the well known mast maker Harry Spencer. When the research *Trivia* was being used for failed to materialise in an America's Cup challenge she was sold, ironically to America. In America *Trivia* fell on hard times; modernised and pushed beyond the endurance of her increasingly fragile hull, she sank. Once raised, she was bought by a descendant of the first owner and returned to Britain. On arrival she was dropped, and suffered yet more damage. Eventually, in early 1990, she was acquired by an Italian enthusiast who returned her to Camper & Nicholsons.

TOP LEFT: *Trivia's wheel and traditional brass binnacle.*
BELOW: *Ash cleats and bronze winches just aft of the mast.*
OPPOSITE: *Awaiting the breeze,* Trivia *is beautifully reflected in the waters off the Italian port of Imperia where a classic yacht regatta is held every other year.*

Trivia's hull was found to be in such poor condition that it required rebuilding completely. Carefully supported, the original hull was used as a template for the new steel frames prior to the replacement of the mahogany planking and renewal of the steamed timbers. Naturally the deck and interior also required complete renewal. The new Columbian pine mast was supplied by her previous skipper Harry Spencer, who has long been established as one of the foremost traditional spar makers.

TOP LEFT: *In the sparsely fitted out main saloon, the warm tones of the mahogany are lightened by the white overhead.*

CENTRE: *Looking aft from the bow showing a little more of the simple open plan interior, which remains spartan in accordance with the racing ethos of the 12 Metre class.*

ABOVE AND BELOW LEFT: *At the 1993 Porto Cervo Veteran Boat Rally.* Trivia *has participated in every phase of the development of the 12 Metre class since she was built; she was also the first classic 12 Metre to rival* Tomahawk *at classic yacht regattas.*

Tomahawk

Year of build	1939
LOD	21.18m/69ft 6in
LWL	13.90m/45ft 7in
Beam	3.62m/11ft 9in
Draft	2.72m/8ft 10in
Designer	Charles E Nicholson
Builder	Camper & Nicholsons, Gosport

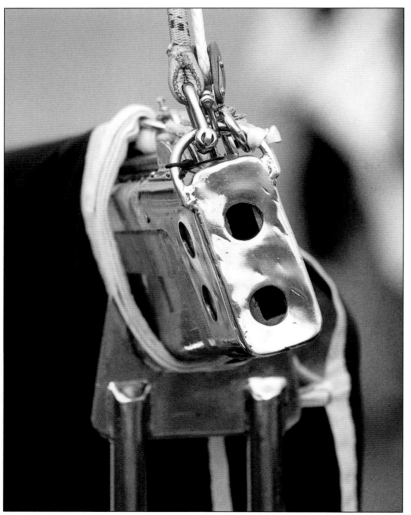

When not racing in the J class, Sir Thomas Sopwith was an avid 12 Metre racer. After the failure of his second America's Cup challenge in 1937, Sopwith returned to 12 Metres, buying *Blue Marlin* (ex *Alanna*) of 1934 vintage. To maintain good sporting relations, Harold Vanderbilt, who had successfully defended the America's Cup in both Sir Thomas Sopwith's challenges, announced that he would bring a 12 Metre yacht to race in Britain for the 1939 season. Twice beaten by Vanderbilt, Sopwith immediately commissioned a new 12 Metre from Charles Nicholson. The resultant *Tomahawk* is the ultimate Nicholson 12 Metre, but when pitted against the Olin Stephens-designed *Vim* she showed again that Nicholson was past absorbing the potential of new technologies. *Vim* had been methodically tank tested and sported an aluminium mast; *Tomahawk* was just an incremental development of Nicholson's previous designs and sported the traditional wooden rig.

TOP LEFT: *The traditional wheel at the after end of the cockpit to which an additional hoop has been fitted.*
BELOW: *The stainless steel boom end fitting.*
OPPOSITE: *Two shots taken just after a start at the 1988 Imperia regatta. Built thirty years apart,* Tomahawk *and* Orion *are both landmarks in Nicholson's career.*

In the aftermath of the Second World War *Tomahawk* lay forgotten in England. It was only with the revival of the America's Cup, now to be competed for by 12 Metres, that British yachtsmen sought to use her as a trial horse. They were too late as she had been sold to Italy, where she has remained ever since. From the ownership of Fiat boss Gianni Angelli, *Tomahawk* passed into the hands of Alberto Rusconi, who undertook a total reconstruction of the frail beauty at the Beconcini yard in La Spezia. When relaunched in 1988, *Tomahawk* was the lone vintage 12 Metre on the Mediterranean classic yacht circuit. Her restoration inspired those of *Trivia*, *Flica II*, *Seven Seas* and *Nyala* but, not satisfied with merely inspiring others, Rusconi went so far as to buy *Vim* so that the old sparring partners might be reunited.

ABOVE AND OPPOSITE: *All the shots on these pages were taken during the Prada Trophy regatta at Porto Santo Stefano in 1998. Here* Tomahawk *is seen match racing against* Nyala, *a 1938 Olin Stephens design. The fresh breeze and flat seas make ideal conditions for these narrow, streamlined yachts which are designed for pure speed.*

The Eight Metres

As with all the classes of the International Rule, C E Nicholson's involvement came relatively late. With the 8 Metre class it was prompted by Camper & Nicholsons' construction in 1909 of *Bryony* for Robert E Froude. A pioneer of tank testing, Froude was employed by the British Admiralty and based at Haslar, a stone's throw from Camper & Nicholsons' Gosport yard. The nature of Froude's expertise and strong interest in yachting had led to his playing a leading role in the development of rating formulae within the Yacht Racing Association. Indeed, he was largely responsible for devising the formula of the International Rule and represented British interests and the international conference that saw its adoption.

Froude's designs for *Bryony* naturally attracted a certain amount of attention and for the detail of her construction he liaised directly with the men building her on Camper & Nicholsons' shop floor. Nicholson was clearly intrigued by the design and more generally by the rise in interest in the 8 Metre class. With no particular customer for an 8 Metre he resorted to speculative construction, as he had so often done previously. At that time Nicholson had not had the opportunity to prove himself under the International Rule and the chance of competing directly with a yacht designed by the person who had conceived the rating formulae must have appealed to him.

Built alongside *Bryony*, Nicholson's *Folly* proved to be the better of the two boats and, although this may have been due in part to Nicholson's expert helmsmanship, the effect was not lost on contemporary observers. As to the 8 Metre class, the situation was more complex and it was some time before it established itself as the premier class in its size range since it was competing with the 6 and 7 Metre classes, to which yacht owners were initially equally attracted.

In the aftermath of the First World War, the 8 Metre class lost position to the 6 Metres, which were chosen as the yachts in which international yacht racing was to be reborn. Both the revived Seawanhaka Cup and the new British America's Cup, which Nicholson had helped institute, were raced for in the 6 Metre Class. Both these events proved exceptionally attractive to Scottish yachtsmen, who not only tended to favour their own designers, of which William Fife was the undisputed leader, but also in 1928 challenged for the Seawanhaka Cup on the condition that it be raced for in the 8 Metre class. The positive implication for the class was clear, but the move came late for Nicholson who had already suggested that the 6 Metre class be renamed the 'Fife Class'.

During the inter-war period Fife outbuilt Nicholson in the 6 Metre class at a ratio of nearly four to one and, whilst the ratio was only two to one in the 8 Metre class, small racing yacht construction was the one area where Nicholson was unable to exert his dominance. In 1924, *Blue Red*, the first of Nicholson's post-First World War 8 Metres, threatened to do his reputation no good at all until he bought her back from her unsuccessful owner and, renaming her *Folly*, gave proof of her abilities.

With the exception of *Feo*, built in 1927, the vast majority of Charles E Nicholson's 8 Metre designs were built after 1928 when his prestige was enhanced by success in the Big Class. Of his two yachts for the 1929 season, *Sagitta*, which he owned jointly with his brother, became one of the yachts most closely associated with Nicholson's racing career on the Solent. Now restored, *Sagitta* has rejoined a near intact fleet of Nicholson's 1930s 8 Metre yachts.

All three of the 8 Metres Nicholson designed for the 1930 season survive in French waters and are maintained in racing trim. Thus *Cutty*, *Suzette* and *Vision* remain the

sparring partners they were always meant to be. Nicholson contributed no further yachts to the class until 1934, when *Cedora* was an isolated order. However she appears to have set a trend, and by 1935 Nicholson was designing a further three 8 Metres. Of these *Wye* is widely regarded as Nicholson's ultimate 8 Metre; maintained in racing condition and based in Stockholm, she has continued to add to an outstanding list of victories. Her near sister *Reality* was shipped out to British Columbia in the 1950s but survives only in name. *Reality*'s hull was allowed to deteriorate to such an extent that it was deemed irreparable, but such was her reputation as a race winner that a new cold-moulded hull was built using the original as a template. Nicholson's final 8 Metre *Rosa* was launched in 1938, bringing an end to his thirty years of designs for the class.

In the wake of the decision to abandon the 12 Metre class for America's Cup racing, the 8 Metre class can claim to be the most successful and long lived of all the Metre classes. In terms of absolute speed, the yachts have relatively small variations which, combined with the incremental pace of change, has tended to keep older boats racing competitively. Now the class is enjoying a wide-scale revival and the long-term prospects are good. A rating basis has been agreed that actively encourages the older yachts in the class to remain true to their original designs and the popularity of the yachts that race for the Coupe Cartier is prompting yet further restorations. The strength of the class is such that it even has a growing gaff-rigged division, which includes the earliest yachts built to the rule. Among these is *Folly*, Nicholson's first 8 Metre class design, which has recently been restored by yacht designer German Frers. However, her stable-mate, the Froude-designed *Bryony*, which more than any other yacht symbolises the origins of the International Rule and the 8 Metre class, is currently unaccounted for. After many years laid up on the Hamble she was moved a few years ago and her whereabouts remain unknown. In a class that has been so successful in preserving its heritage, assuring the long-term future of *Bryony* must now assume a high priority.

Folly was the first 8 Metre hull designed and built by Charles Nicholson in 1909 as his personal yacht. Today she is perfectly restored and in June 2000 she was the oldest yacht racing the 8 Metre World Championship in Porto Santo, Italy.

THIS PAGE: Folly *with her gaff rig, a view of the cockpit, a detail of the deck and the bowsprit, the work on the leather covering, the rings on the mast.*

FACING PAGE: *Two images of* Folly *racing in Porto Santo Stefano with twenty knots of wind. At the helm is her current owner German Frers.*

Many of the 8 Metre class yachts designed by Charles E Nicholson still participate regularly in the World Championships organised by the class association. Of all the Metre classes, the 8 Metre class is the most active and well supported.

TOP LEFT: Feo *designed and built in 1927.*
BELOW LEFT: Suzette *of 1930 racing on lake Geneva in 1998.*
ABOVE: Blue Red *was built in 1924, she is seen here racing at the 1993 Nioulargue regatta.*
FACING PAGE BELOW: Vision *seen under spinnaker and* Cutty Tou *close-hauled. Both were launched for the 1930 season and remain rivals to this day.*